ALL ABOUT® Reading

The program that takes the struggle out of reading

Level 1

Second Edition

by Marie Rippel

Copyright © 2017, 2016 by All About® Learning Press, Inc.
Previous editions copyright © 2011-2015
Printed in the United States of America

Second Edition
v.2.0.1

All About® Learning Press, Inc.
615 Commerce Loop
Eagle River, WI 54521

ISBN 978-1-935197-62-1

Editor: Renée LaTulippe
Cover Design: Dave LaTulippe

The *All About® Reading* Level 1 Teacher's Manual is part of the *All About® Reading* program.

For more books in this series, go to www.AllAboutReading.com.

Contents

3 Appendices

1

Preparing for Level 1

What Do You Need?

In addition to this Teacher's Manual, you will need the following items:

1. Student Packet

The Student Packet contains:

- *Blast Off to Reading!* activity book
- Phonogram Cards and Word Cards
- Viewfinder Bookmark

2. Interactive Kit

The Interactive Kit contains:

- Letter Tiles
- Divider Cards
- *Phonogram Sounds* app
- Reading Review Box (Deluxe Kit)
- Stickers for the Progress Chart (Deluxe Kit)
- Tote Bag (Deluxe Kit)

(If you did not get the Reading Review Box, you will need an index card box.)

3. Readers

- *Run, Bug, Run!*
- *The Runt Pig*
- *Cobweb the Cat*

(This Teacher's Manual must be used with the Second Edition of these readers, which contain additional stories.)

4. Common Craft Materials

- Crayons, scissors, glue, tape, stapler
- Two small baggies in which to store your letter tiles

5. 2' x 3' Magnetic White Board

A magnetic white board is optional, but highly recommended.

6. Optional Items

If your student enjoyed working with Ziggy in the *All About Reading* Pre-reading program, or if you are working with a student six or under, you may wish to add the book of games called *Reading Games with Ziggy the Zebra.*

If you are working with a younger student, you may wish to use a puppet to help you "teach" the lessons and keep student interest high.

What You Should Know about This Program

First of all, you can do this! *All About Reading* is a scripted, open-and-go program developed for busy parents, teachers, and tutors who want to teach reading in the most effective way possible. This program doesn't require long periods of study, you don't have to develop your own lesson plans, and you don't have to stress over what to teach next—because everything is laid out for you, step by step. You'll get solid grounding in how to teach reading without being overwhelmed.

Your student will be actively involved in the learning process. This is a truly multisensory program; your student will learn through sight, sound, and touch. Everything is taught in context, and your student will apply what he has learned right away. Your student will be engaged in thinking, processing, comparing, and learning.

Students who use the *All About Reading* method tend to feel a sense of excitement in learning. And they should! They are learning how to think, explore, and grow in their abilities. They feel successful as they see continual progress.

There are no gaps in this program. Your student will be taught everything he or she needs to know about reading, so no guessing is required. Each new concept builds upon the previous one, and no steps are skipped.

There are five key components of reading—and our program teaches all of them thoroughly. These five components are:

1. Phonological Awareness
2. Phonics and Decoding
3. Fluency
4. Vocabulary
5. Comprehension

All About Reading **is a mastery-based program.** As such, the levels don't correspond to grade levels. In mastery-based learning, students master one concept before moving on to a more advanced concept, regardless of age or grade level.

Most importantly, *All About Reading* **is committed to results.** The *All About Reading* program has a very focused mission: to enable you to teach your student to read while guaranteeing retention and enjoyment. Our approach to reading focuses on enabling students to become confident, fluent readers who can absorb and retain new information.

If you ever have a question as you are teaching, please feel free to contact us at support@allaboutlearningpress.com or 715-477-1976. We're here to help!

Is Your Student in the Right Level?

Starting Level 1 of *All About Reading* is an exciting time for you and your student. Together, you'll explore fascinating new concepts—including phonograms, counting syllables, and reading stories—and begin to establish a firm foundation for a lifetime of reading. But before your student begins Level 1, be sure he or she is comfortable with these vital prerequisite concepts.

Your student should display **letter knowledge**.

- ☐ Your student can recite the alphabet song.

- ☐ Your student recognizes the capital letters. If you ask your student to point to an <u>M</u>, he can do it.

- ☐ Your student recognizes the lowercase letters. If you ask your student to point to an <u>r</u>, he can do it.

Your student should display **print awareness**.

- ☐ Your student knows the proper way to hold a book.

- ☐ Your student understands that books are read from cover to back.

- ☐ Your student understands that sentences are read from left to right.

- ☐ Your student knows that words on the page can be read.

Your student should display **listening comprehension**.

- ☐ Your student is able to retell a familiar story in his own words.

- ☐ Your student can answer simple questions about a story.

- ☐ Your student asks questions (*Why did the elephant laugh?*) during read-alouds.

Your student should display **phonological awareness**.

- ☐ Your student can rhyme. If you say *bat*, your student can come up with a rhyming word like *hat*.

- ☐ Your student understands word boundaries. If you say the sentence *Don't let the cat out*, your student is able to separate the sentence into five individual words.

- ☐ Your student can clap syllables. If you say *dog*, your student knows to clap once. If you say *umbrella*, your student knows to clap three times.

☐ Your student can blend sounds to make a word. If you say the sounds *sh...eep*, your student responds with the word *sheep*.

☐ Your student can identify the beginning sound in a word. If you ask your student to say the first sound in *pig*, your student is able to respond with the sound /p/.

☐ Your student can identify the ending sound in a word. If you ask your student to say the last sound in the word *jam*, your student is able to respond with the sound /m/.

Your student should display **motivation to read**.

Use your intuition to understand if your student is motivated to begin reading. The following are all signs that your student is motivated to read and has achieved the understanding that reading is fun.

☐ Does your student enjoy being read to, at least for short periods of time?

☐ Does your student pretend to read or write?

☐ Does your student frequently request read-aloud time and show a general enthusiasm for books?

How did your student do?

- If all or most of the boxes are checked, then your student is ready for *All About Reading* Level 1!

- If there are some missing checkmarks, then you've identified the areas that you should work on with your student.

- It is surprisingly easy to fill in these gaps in an engaging way with the *All About Reading* Pre-reading program.

Is Your Student in the Right Level?

Preview the Teacher's Manual

As you flip through the Teacher's Manual, you'll notice that all the lessons are laid out for you, step by step. You'll also notice that there are two types of lessons.

1. "New concept" lessons. In these lessons, your student will learn new phonograms and words. You can see an example of a typical "new concept" lesson in Lesson 1 on page 31.

2. "Read a story" lessons. In these lessons, your student will practice concepts taught in the previous lesson by reading a story. Vocabulary and comprehension strategies are emphasized. You can see an example of a typical "read a story" lesson in Lesson 3 on page 49.

Most lessons consist of five parts:

1. **Before You Begin.** In this section, you may be prompted to preview the sounds of the phonograms you will be teaching, place new tiles on the magnetic white board, or get a quick introduction to new terminology. This section never takes more than a couple of minutes, and after reading it, you will be well equipped to teach the lesson confidently.

2. **Review.** This section will prompt you to begin your lessons with a review of previously taught concepts. You will need your student's Reading Review Box for this part of the lesson.

3. **New Teaching.** This is the hands-on, multisensory portion of the lesson. Your student will work with the letter tiles and activity sheets while completing comprehension, vocabulary, and fluency exercises.

4. **Read-Aloud Time.** This section is a friendly reminder to fit in twenty minutes of read-aloud time every day. Modeling good reading habits for your student is a fundamental part of the *All About Reading* curriculum.

5. **Track Your Progress.** This is where you will record your student's progression on the Progress Chart.

Flip through the remaining lessons. You'll see that some lessons are longer and others are shorter. Depending on your student and how much time you have allocated, you may sometimes be able to cover more than one lesson in one sitting. If your student thoroughly understands a lesson and you sense that he is ready for the next challenge, move straight into the next lesson.

If you are working with a younger student, you may only complete part of a lesson. That's okay! Simply mark your place in the lesson plan. The next day, start your lesson with a quick review and then pick up where you left off.

Don't feel like you must push through an entire lesson if your student isn't ready. Do what is best for your student.

Preview the Activity Book

The *Blast Off to Reading!* activity book contains:

- Progress Chart
- Read-Aloud Record
- Activity Sheets
- Warm-Up Sheets
- Practice Sheets
- Certificate of Completion

The pages in the activity book are perforated for easy removal. The lesson plans in the Teacher's Manual will tell you which pages you need for each lesson.

Let's take a quick look at each part of the activity book.

The Progress Chart

The Progress Chart can be found on page 5 of the activity book.

This chart is a motivating part of the lessons for many students because it is a visual reminder of the progress they have made toward reading independently.

Remove the chart on the perforation and decide where to place it. Choose a prominent place like a bulletin board, the refrigerator, the back of a door, or another easily accessible area. Your student may wish to color or decorate the chart.

After each lesson has been completed, have your student color in or place a sticker over the next star on the chart.

The Read-Aloud Record

The Read-Aloud Record can be found on page 7 of the activity book.

Toward the end of each lesson, you will be prompted to read to your student for twenty minutes from a book of your choice. The Read-Aloud Record will help keep you on track with your daily reading and serve as a fun reminder of all the books you and your student have read together.

The daily read-aloud time may seem like a simple part of the reading lessons, but it's actually one of the most important components. While your student is listening to good books, he'll also be:

- gaining important background knowledge on a wide variety of subjects;
- developing a larger vocabulary; and
- hearing a variety of language patterns.

Your student's reading comprehension will be much higher because you've given him these huge benefits through daily read-aloud time.

Here are some things to think about as you plan ahead for read-aloud time:

- **Figure out the best time of day for your read-aloud time.**
  You might find it easiest to connect read-aloud time to something else that you already do every day. It often works well to schedule it after lunch, recess, or a specific class. If you are a parent, bedtime is a natural time for enjoying books together.

- **Gather a variety of books, both fiction and non-fiction.**
  To keep interest high, look for books related to your student's specific interests and hobbies. You can also stimulate new interests by choosing read-alouds on topics that are completely new to your student.

- **Decide how you will minimize distractions.**
  At home, turn off the TV, computer, and telephone. Clear away competing toys and games. If you have a wiggly student, you can help him concentrate on the story by allowing him to play quietly while you read. Some students will be fine just holding a toy, while others might prefer to build with blocks, knead clay, or color quietly. For some students, it is easier to stay in one place and pay attention to what you are reading if they don't have to remain perfectly still.

The Activity Sheets

The activity sheets are very motivating for most kids. They provide a variety of ways to practice what they've just learned in the lesson. Flashcards and word banks have their place, but it is nice to break out of the "serious" learning and have a little fun applying it!

Take a look at the activity called "Word Match" on page 9 of the activity book. When you get to Lesson 1, the lesson plans will prompt you to cut out the word cards from the bottom of the page. You'll place the word cards in a pile, and your student will choose a card and place it under the matching picture with the word facing up. He will then answer a couple of comprehension questions about the words.

If you are working with an older student who doesn't need the additional practice for a certain concept, or who doesn't want to do "kid" activities, feel free to skip that particular activity sheet. But you may find that even adult learners enjoy the mental break that the activity sheets provide.

For the activity sheets, you will need these basic supplies:
- scissors
- stapler
- crayons, colored pencils, or markers (optional)
- pencil

The Practice Sheets

Take a look at the Practice Sheet on page 15 of the activity book.

The Practice Sheets give your student practice reading words that reflect newly learned concepts. Most of the Practice Sheets contain three sections: New Words, Phrases, and Sentences.

The Sentences section includes short phrases like *Dad had*, and longer sentences like *Dad had a bad rib*.

This type of practice is called *phrased reading*. Phrasing is important for fluency; fluent readers are able to phrase, or break text into meaningful chunks.

If your student does not need practice with phrasing, feel free to skip the shorter phrases and have your student read just the full sentences.

Over time, the Practice Sheets will help your student move from sounding out words letter by letter to instant recognition of words. This change usually happens gradually, so don't expect perfection at first.

Here are some tips to help you get the most benefit out of the Practice Sheets:

1. **Place the sheet directly in front of your student.**

2. **Read across the page from left to right** to reinforce proper eye movements. Don't read down the columns.

3. **Stop before your student fatigues.** You might not complete the Practice Sheet all in one day, depending on your student's age and attention span.

4. **Would your student benefit from reviewing the Practice Sheet several times?** If so, repeat the exercise several days in a row.

5. **On the other hand, don't overwhelm your student with *too* much practice.** It is important to find the right balance for your individual student. Some students desperately need the practice provided, while others (especially younger students) are better served by reading every other line, or every third line.

For more tips on using the Practice Sheets, see Appendix F.

The Warm-Up Sheets

You can find an example of a Warm-Up Sheet on page 19 of the activity book.

The Warm-Up Sheets are used just before reading a new story and contain words and phrases your student is about to encounter. Although all the words in the stories are completely decodable, these warm-up exercises give your student a little extra practice so he doesn't start reading "cold." Just as warming up our muscles before exercising is beneficial, warming up the brain before jumping right into a story helps your student be more successful.

The illustrations on the Warm-Up Sheets are used during short pre-reading vocabulary discussions.

Preview the Activity Book

Preview the Readers

All About Reading Level 1 includes three readers that are 100% decodable. *Run, Bug, Run!* is first used in Lesson 3. *The Runt Pig* is first used in Lesson 25. *Cobweb the Cat* is first used in Lesson 41.

Your student will read one or two stories in approximately every other lesson.

The first time a student reads a story is called a "cold reading." The student may read choppily, one word at a time. This is normal because the student is working very hard at decoding many of the individual words. Don't expect smooth reading during the cold reading.

Most students benefit from "repeated readings"—that is, reading the story a second or even third time. You'll find that during the repeated reading, your student will read more fluently and with better understanding. Since every student's needs will vary, these repeated readings are not scheduled in the lesson plans. Be sure to make time for them!

The Teacher's Manual provides comprehension questions and activity sheets for each story. If you feel your student would benefit from further activities, refer to Appendix I: List of Comprehension Activities.

If your student is having difficulty reading the stories, refer to Appendix J: If Your Student Struggles with the Stories.

Organize the Manipulatives

There are three things left to do to prepare for your first lesson: get your letter tiles ready, set up your Reading Review Box, and preview the *Phonogram Sounds* app.

Get Your Letter Tiles Ready

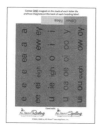

Take out the laminated Letter Tiles sheets. Separate the letter tiles and labels on the perforations.

Apply the magnets to the back of the letter tiles. Stick one magnet on the back of each letter tile and two magnets on the back of each label. (Skip this step if you will be using the letter tiles on a tabletop instead of a magnetic white board.)

Next, prepare two small plastic baggies. Label one bag *Level 1* and the other bag *Levels 2-4*. Place the following tiles and labels in your *Level 1* baggie:

- two sets of letters <u>a</u> to <u>z</u>
- letter tiles <u>th</u>, <u>sh</u>, <u>ch</u>, <u>ck</u>, <u>ng</u>, <u>nk</u>, and third <u>s</u>
- Consonant Teams label

Put the remaining tiles and labels, including the blank ones, in the *Levels 2-4* baggie. Store the baggie in your *All About Reading* tote bag or another safe place.

Set Up Your Magnetic White Board

You'll be using the letter tiles in every "new concept" lesson. Set up your magnetic white board with one set of letter tiles <u>a</u> to <u>z</u>, as shown below.

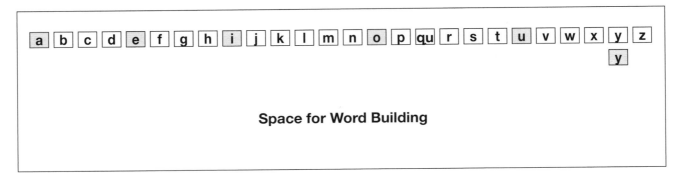

Space for Word Building

Notes:
- Use both the blue and the red <u>y</u> tiles in this initial setup.
- Store the remaining letters in your *Level 1* baggie.
- There is no tile for letter <u>q</u>. Instead, there is a letter tile containing <u>qu</u>, since <u>q</u> is always followed by a <u>u</u> in English words.

<u>Answers to **Common Questions**</u>

What do the different colors mean?
- Blue tiles are consonants and consonant teams.
- Red tiles are vowels and vowel teams.
- Purple tiles are for the sound of /er/.
- Yellow tiles are for Bossy R combinations.
- Green tiles are for alternate spellings of /sh/: <u>ti</u>, <u>ci</u>, <u>si</u>.
- Orange tiles are for miscellaneous symbols and letters.

You'll learn about each category when you get to it in the lessons.

Why are there two different <u>y</u>'s?
- <u>Y</u> can be a consonant or a vowel, depending on the word.
- When it is a consonant, it says /y/.
- When it is a vowel, it can say /ĭ/, /ī/, or /ē/.

What will happen with the other letter tiles that are left in my *Level 1* baggie?
- Starting in Lesson 18, we will gradually add the remaining letter tiles to the board.
- Keep the baggie in a safe place (such as your reading tote bag) until the tiles are needed.
- To see what the board will look like by the end of Level 1, see Appendix L.

What if I don't have a magnetic white board?
A magnetic white board makes it easier and faster to set up for your reading lessons, but if you don't have a magnetic white board, you can set up the letter tiles right on your table. The lesson plans are

worded as if you are using a magnetic white board, but please know that you can do exactly the same thing on your tabletop.

What do all these funny marks and symbols mean?

As a shorthand way to represent the sounds of letters in this Teacher's Manual, we use slashes. For example, /m/ stands for the spoken sound *mmm* as in *monkey*.

You will also see two other sound symbols:

- A straight line above a letter, as in /ā/, represents the long vowel sound. This symbol is called a *macron*.
- A "smile" above a letter, as in /ă/, represents the short vowel sound. This symbol is called a *breve*.

For a complete list of letter sounds and key words, please see Appendix B.

Prepare Your Reading Review Box

The Reading Review Box organizes your flashcards so review time can be productive for your student. Every lesson, except the first one, starts with review. Whether you use our custom Reading Review Box or your own index card box, follow the instructions below to set it up.

1. **Place the divider cards in your box.** The divider cards are numbered 1-6 so you can be sure to get them in the correct order. Foam spacers are also provided to allow the cards to stand upright. As you need more room for cards, simply remove a foam spacer.

2. **Locate the yellow Phonogram Cards** in the Student Packet. Separate the perforated cards and place them behind the yellow tabbed divider called *Phonogram Cards–Future Lessons*.

3. **Locate the green Word Cards** in the Student Packet. Separate the perforated cards and place them behind the green tabbed divider called *Word Cards–Future Lessons*.

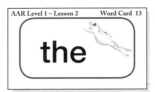

4. Preview the Leap Word Cards. Take a look at Word Card 13. See the frog?

We use the frog graphic to indicate high-frequency words that either don't follow the normal rules or that contain phonograms that your student hasn't practiced yet. Your student will be "leaping ahead" to learn these words as sight words.

There are eleven Leap Words in Level 1, and the first one is taught in Lesson 2. Several techniques will be used to help your student remember these Leap Words:

- The frog graphic acts as a visual reminder to your student that the word is being treated as a sight word.

- Leap Word Cards are kept behind the Review divider in your student's Reading Review Box until your student has achieved instant recognition of the word.

- Leap Words frequently appear on the Practice Sheets.

- Leap Words are used frequently in the readers.

- If a Leap Word causes your student trouble, have your student use a light-colored crayon to circle the part of the word that doesn't say what your student expects it to say. Help your student see that Leap Words generally have just one or two letters that are troublesome, while the rest of the letters say their regular sounds and follow normal patterns.

For the complete list of Leap Words taught in Level 1, see Appendix M.

Preview the Letter Sounds

In Level 1, we'll be teaching the sounds of letters a to z and th, sh, ch, ck, ng, and nk.

You can preview these sounds with the *Phonogram Sounds* app.

Scan the QR code below to download the *Phonogram Sounds* app.

- **Download the app for your computer, tablet, or phone at** www.allaboutlearningpress.com/phonogram-sounds-app or scan the QR code. *(Note: If you'd prefer not to download the app, a CD-ROM version is available for purchase.)*

- **Open the program and click on the letter m, which is the first letter you will be teaching in Lesson 1.** You'll hear the sound of the letter m: /m/.

- **Next, click on the letter s, which is the second letter you will be teaching.** You'll hear both sounds for the letter s: /s/–/z/. In Lesson 1, you will only be teaching the first sound, /s/. Later, in Lesson 12, you will teach the second sound. The same is true for all of the letter tiles in Level 1 that have more than one sound: first we teach the most common sound, and within a short period of time, we teach the remaining sounds.

- **If you are unsure about how to pronounce the sounds of the letters** at any point in the program, refer to the *Phonogram Sounds* app.

You can also find a chart of the phonograms in Appendix B of this Teacher's Manual.

For letters with more than one sound, you may choose to teach all the sounds up front, and that is perfectly acceptable. Simply teach the multiple sounds, and then let your student know that you will be working with the first sound for the rest of the lesson. You'll work with the remaining sounds in future lessons.

The short vowel sounds are generally more difficult for students to remember, so when the vowels are taught, we add hand motions to make them more memorable. For example, the hand motion for the sound of /ă/ as in *apple* is to cup your hand as if you are holding an apple.

How Much Time Should I Spend on Reading?

All About Reading lessons are designed so that you can work at your student's pace. Following are general guidelines.

Spend 20 minutes per day teaching reading.

I recommend spending about 20 minutes per day, five days a week, on reading instruction, but you can adjust this if necessary for early readers or for older remedial students.

It can be helpful to set a timer. When 20 minutes are up, mark the spot in the lesson where you stopped. When you begin teaching the next day, briefly review some of the daily review cards, and then begin in the Teacher's Manual wherever you left off previously.

Short daily lessons are much more effective than longer, less frequent lessons. Your student's attention is less likely to wander, and you can accomplish more when your student is actively engaged in the lesson.

If you aren't done with the lesson when the 20 minutes are up, don't worry! This next tip is for you.

Lessons often take more than one day to complete.

Please know that the lessons in *All About Reading* are **not** meant to be completed in one day.

In fact, some lessons may take a week or more to finish. A number of variables including your student's age, attention span, prior experience, the difficulty of the concept being taught, and the length of the stories all play a part in how quickly a lesson can be completed.

And after the formal lesson, it will be time for some great read-alouds!

In addition to the lessons, read aloud to your student for 20 minutes per day.

Reading aloud to your student is one of the most important things you can do to promote future reading ability. In fact, this is such an important part of the program that it is actually added as a reminder at the end of every lesson.

Reading aloud for 20 minutes a day may not seem like a lot, but the cumulative effect cannot be overstated. By reading aloud for just 20 minutes a day over a five-year period, your student will have the advantage of 600 hours of read-alouds. That equates to huge gains in vocabulary, comprehension, and background information.

When you combine 20 minutes of direct reading instruction with 20 minutes of read-aloud time, you can rest assured that you are providing your student with the very best opportunity for long-term reading success.

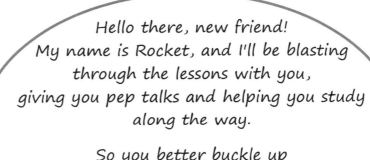

2

Complete Step-by-Step Lesson Plans

Lesson 1 - Letters M, S, P, and A

This lesson will introduce the blending procedure and the terms *vowels* and *consonants*, and teach words containing the letters m̲, s̲, p̲, and a̲.

You will need:
☐ Phonogram Cards 1-4   ☐ Word Cards 1-3
☐ Blast Off to Reading! page 9   ☐ Progress Chart

Before You Begin

At the beginning of many of the lessons, you will find a "Before You Begin" section enclosed in a box. Review these instructions before you begin the lesson.

The actual lesson plan you will teach to your student begins *after* the boxed section.

Preview the Sounds of the Letters

The four letters in today's lesson were chosen because their sounds are easy for students to learn and can be used right away to form simple words.

m The letter m̲ says /m/ as in *moon*.

s The letter s̲ can say two sounds:
- /s/ as in *sun* (taught in this lesson)
- /z/ as in *has* (taught in Lesson 12)

p The letter p̲ says /p/ as in *pig*. Be sure that you and your student don't add /uh/ to the end of the sound, as in /puh/.

a The letter a̲ can say three sounds:
- /ă/ as in *apple*, known as the short sound (taught in this lesson)
- /ā/ as in *acorn*, known as the long sound (taught in Lesson 44)
- /ah/ as in *father* (taught in Lesson 44)

Preview the Hand Motion for Letter A

Tip! To further cement this sound in your student's mind, take a bite out of the pretend apple with a loud crunch! The more dramatic you make this activity, the better your student will remember it.

Level 1 - Lesson 1   Phonogram Card 4

a

Notice the hand on the card for a̲. This indicates that there is a hand motion that goes along with the sound. Your student will pretend to hold an apple in his hand as he says "/ă/–/ă/–apple."

Vowel sounds are usually more difficult for students to learn. We make it easier by adding hand motions and teaching only one new vowel sound at a time.

Before You Begin
(continued)

Listen to the *Phonogram Sounds* app for a demonstration of the phonogram sounds.

Preview Vowels and Consonants

Set up the letter tiles in alphabetical order before the start of the lesson, as shown on page 22.

a b c d e f g h i j k l m n o p qu r s t u v w x y z
y

Your student will learn that the red tiles are vowels and the blue tiles are consonants.

If you are using *Reading Games with Ziggy the Zebra*, you can play "Apples for Ziggy" to reinforce the concept of vowels and consonants.

Preview the Blending Procedure

In the first twenty-three lessons, your student will be blending and reading words with the Consonant-Vowel-Consonant pattern such as *mat*, *run*, and *did*. These words are sometimes referred to as CVC words, and the vowel sound is always short. Although the scripted lessons will walk you through the blending procedure, you might also refer to Appendix C for an overview of the process.

Note that learning to blend can take time! Don't be concerned if it takes several lessons for your student to grasp the concept of blending. We'll review blending in each "new concept" lesson, so your student will get plenty of practice.

New Teaching

Teach New Letter Sounds

Hold up the Phonogram Card for the letter <u>m</u>.

"This letter says /m/."

"Now it's your turn. What does this letter say?" *Student says /m/.*

Hold up the Phonogram Card for the letter <u>s</u>.

"This letter says /s/."

"Your turn. What does this letter say?" *Student says /s/.*

Hold up the Phonogram Card for the letter <u>p</u>.

"This letter says /p/."

"Your turn." *Student says /p/.*

Hold up the Phonogram Card for the letter <u>a</u>.

"This letter says /ă/."

Cup your hand as if you are holding an apple. "When we say /ă/, let's pretend that we are holding an apple. Say the sound of <u>a</u> like this: /ă/–/ă/–apple." *Student pretends to hold an apple and says /ă/–/ă/–apple.*

Point to the hand symbol on the card. "This hand will remind you that there is a hand motion for <u>a</u>."

 Shuffle the cards and review them several times.

 File these flashcards behind the **Phonogram Cards Review** divider in your student's Reading Review Box. The cards will be reviewed at the beginning of the next lesson.

Now practice the same sounds using the letter tiles. Pull these four letter tiles down into your workspace.

Point to each one in random order and ask your student to tell you the sound that each tile makes. Practice until your student can say the sound of each letter accurately.

New Teaching
(continued)

Tip! Be sure your student uses the pointer finger of his dominant hand for this exercise.

Demonstrate How to Blend Sounds

Build the word *map* with letter tiles. m a p

"Watch while I show you how we sound out words."

"I touch each letter tile in order, and I say the sound of that letter."

Touch the <u>m</u> and say /*m*/.

Touch the <u>a</u> and say /*ă*/.

Touch the <u>p</u> and say /*p*/.

Now go back to the beginning of the word and blend the sounds together as follows.

Slide your finger under the letters <u>m</u>-<u>a</u> and say /*mă*/.

Start at the beginning of the word again. Slide your finger under the letters <u>m</u>-<u>a</u>-<u>p</u> and say *map* slowly.

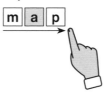

Tip! When your student reads the word in this last step, you may need to prompt him to say the word "fast like we talk."

Finally, read the word *map* at a normal pace, as we do when we speak.

Using the same procedure for blending, have your student sound out the word *Sam*.

s a m

Lesson 1: Letters M, S, P, and A

New Teaching
(continued)

You may wish to point out to your student that *Sam* and *Pam* are names, and when they are in print, they are capitalized. You may demonstrate by writing the names on paper, or turn to page 9 in the *Blast Off* activity book and point out the names shown at the bottom of the page.

Play "Change the Word"

Leave the word *Sam* on the board. | s | a | m |

"I'm going to change the first letter of this word."

"What does this new word say?" Encourage your student to sound out the new word. *Pam.*

Build the word *sap.* | s | a | p |

"Sound out this word." *Student sounds out the word* sap.

Change the first letter to form the word *map.*

"What does this new word say?" *Student sounds out the word* map.

Teach Vowels and Consonants

"Some of the letter tiles are red. Say the names of the letters on the red tiles." *A̲, e̲, i̲, o̲, u̲, and y̲.*

"The red tiles are *vowels*: a̲, e̲, i̲, o̲, u̲, and sometimes y̲."

"The blue tiles are *consonants*. C̲ is a consonant. P̲ is a consonant." Point to the letter tiles as you mention them.

"Can you tell me some other consonants?" *Student names some consonants.*

Point to the two y̲ tiles. | y | y |

"The letter y̲ can be a vowel or a consonant. That's why we have a red y̲ and a blue y̲."

New Teaching

(continued)

Don't Forget

If you are working with an older student, feel free to skip any of the activity sheets that your student wouldn't enjoy.

Complete Activity Sheet

Word Match

Remove page 9 from the *Blast Off* activity book.

Cut out the word cards from the bottom of the page.

Have your student place the appropriate card under the matching picture.

Explain that names start with a capital letter.

"Which of these words are names?" *Pam and Sam.*

"Which of these words rhyme?" *Pam and Sam, map and sap.*

Practice Reading Words

Have your student practice reading the words on Word Cards 1-3.

If your student can't automatically read these words by sight, he shouldn't guess at them. Instead, encourage your student to decode words using the blending procedure taught in this lesson.

File these flashcards behind the **Word Cards Review** divider in your student's Reading Review Box. The cards will be reviewed at the beginning of the next lesson.

Read-Aloud Time

Read a Story or Poem

Read aloud to your student for twenty minutes.

Lesson 1: Letters M, S, P, and A

Track Your Progress

Mark the Progress Chart

If you haven't already done so, remove page 5 from the activity book.

After each lesson has been completed, have your student color in or place a sticker over that lesson number on the Progress Chart.

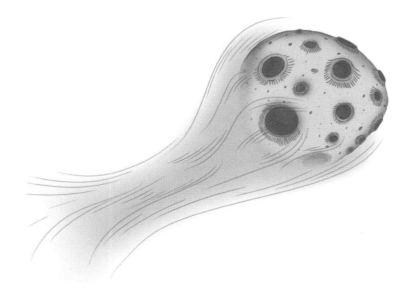

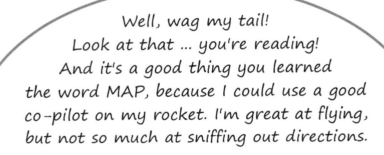

Well, wag my tail!
Look at that ... you're reading!
And it's a good thing you learned
the word MAP, because I could use a good
co-pilot on my rocket. I'm great at flying,
but not so much at sniffing out directions.

So what do you say?
If you're ready for Lesson 2,
let's pack up our gear
and head for the stars!

Lesson 1: Letters M, S, P, and A

Lesson 2 - Letters N, T, B, and J

This lesson will teach words containing the letters <u>n</u>, <u>t</u>, <u>b</u>, and <u>j</u>, as well as the Leap Word <u>the</u>.

You will need: ☐ Phonogram Cards 5-8   ☐ Word Cards 4-13
                ☐ Blast Off to Reading! pages 11-15

Before You Begin

Preview the Sounds of the Letters

n The letter <u>n</u> says /n/ as in *nest*. If your student has difficulty discriminating between the sounds of /n/ and /m/, have him watch your lips as you pronounce the sounds.

t The letter <u>t</u> says /t/ as in *tent*. Be sure that you and your student don't add /uh/ to the end of the sound, as in /tuh/.

b The letter <u>b</u> says /b/ as in *bat*. It is impossible to say /b/ in isolation without any trace of /uh/ at the end, but clip the /uh/ as short as possible.

j The letter <u>j</u> says /j/ as in *jam*. Be sure that you and your student don't add /uh/ to the end of the sound, as in /juh/.

 Listen to the *Phonogram Sounds* app for a demonstration of the phonogram sounds.

 If you are using *Reading Games with Ziggy the Zebra*, you can play "Ziggy at the Market" as a fun way to practice the Phonogram Cards.

Look Ahead to the Review Section

You'll see that each lesson starts with a Review section. Review covers two main areas: Phonograms and Word Cards.

Before You Begin
(continued)

You'll use the Reading Review Box to keep track of what has been mastered and what still needs to be reviewed. If your student knows the Phonogram or Word Card without prompting and you feel that the card has been mastered, place the card behind the **Mastered** divider. If the card has not yet been mastered, place it behind the **Review** divider so it can be reviewed again in the next lesson.

How do you know when your student has mastered a Phonogram Card?

If your student...
- says the pure, clipped sound without adding /uh/ at the end—for example, he says /p/, not /puh/;
- responds quickly and easily when you hold up the card;
- does not hesitate to think of the answer; and
- you have no doubt that your student knows the card thoroughly...

...then that Phonogram Card is mastered! Move it behind the Mastered divider.

How do you know when your student has mastered a Word Card?

If your student is able to read the word on the card without having to sound it out, then you can consider that Word Card as mastered.

Preview the Practice Sheets

Over time, using the Practice Sheets will help your student move from sounding out words letter by letter to being able to instantly recognize words. This change usually happens gradually, so don't expect perfection at first.

Here are some tips to help you get the most benefit out of the Practice Sheets:

1. **Place the sheet directly in front of your student.**

2. **Read across the page from left to right** to reinforce proper eye movements. Don't read down the columns.

Before You Begin
(continued)

3. **The viewfinder bookmark can help your student focus on individual words.** Either run the top edge of the bookmark under the line of text, or center the word or phrase in the cutout area.

cobweb

4. **Stop before your student fatigues.** You might not complete the Practice Sheets all in one day, depending on your student's age and attention span.

5. **Would your student benefit from reviewing the Practice Sheets several times?** If so, repeat the exercise several days in a row.

6. **On the other hand, don't overwhelm your beginning reader with *too much practice* with the Practice Sheets.** It is important to find the right balance for your individual student. Some students desperately need the practice provided, while others (especially younger students) are better served by reading every other line, or every third line.

See Appendix F for more tips on using the Practice Sheets.

Remember that this is hard work for most beginning readers, especially if they are still at the stage of sounding out each word. Reward effort with words of praise!

Review

Review the Phonogram Cards that are behind the Review divider in your student's Reading Review Box. Show the card to your student and have him say the sound. If necessary, remind your student of the sound.

Review the Word Cards that are behind the Review divider in your student's Reading Review Box. If your student has difficulty reading the word, build the word with letter tiles and have your student sound it out using the procedure shown in Appendix C: Full Blending Procedure.

Ask your student to point to some vowels and some consonants.

New Teaching

Teach New Letter Sounds

 Hold up the Phonogram Card for the letter n̲.

"This letter says /n/."

"Now it's your turn. What does this letter say?" *Student says /n/.*

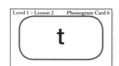 Hold up the Phonogram Card for the letter t̲.

"This letter says /t/."

"Your turn. What does this letter say?" *Student says /t/.*

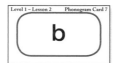 Hold up the Phonogram Card for the letter b̲.

"This letter says /b/."

"Your turn." *Student says /b/.*

 Hold up the Phonogram Card for the letter j̲.

"This letter says /j/."

"Your turn." *Student says /j/.*

File the Phonogram Cards behind the Review divider of the Reading Review Box.

Now practice the same sounds using the letter tiles. Pull these four letter tiles down into your workspace.

Point to each one in random order and ask your student to tell you the sound that each tile makes. Practice until your student can say the sound of each letter accurately.

 File the four new Phonogram Cards behind the **Review** divider and review them at the beginning of the next lesson. Doing so will help you better determine if your student has really mastered the phonogram.

It often seems as if a student has mastered a new card during the reading lesson, but when you revisit that card in a day or two, it becomes obvious that he really hasn't.

It often takes multiple sessions to master a new phonogram.

New Teaching
(continued)

Practice Commonly Confused Letters

Pull down the <u>m</u> and <u>n</u> letter tiles. Randomly dictate /m/ and /n/ to test whether your student can distinguish between the two sounds and choose the correct letter tile.

If your student has difficulty telling the difference between /m/ and /n/, have him watch your mouth as you say the sounds.

Blend Sounds with Letter Tiles

Build the word *pan* with letter tiles.   p a n

"I'll sound out this first word, and then you'll sound out the next word."

Touch the <u>p</u> and say /p/.

Touch the <u>a</u> and say /ă/.

Touch the <u>n</u> and say /n/.

Now go back to the beginning of the word and blend the sounds together as follows.

Slide your finger under the letters <u>p</u>-<u>a</u> and say /pă/.

New Teaching

(continued)

Start at the beginning of the word again. Slide your finger under the letters p-a-n and say *pan* slowly.

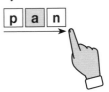

> You may want to point out to your student that *pan* and *nap* contain the same letters, just in a different order.
>
> **Tip!**

Finally, read the word *pan* at a normal pace, as we do when we speak.

Using the same procedure for blending, have your student sound out the word *nap*.

| n | a | p |

Play "Change the Word"

Leave the word *nap* on the board. | n | a | p |

"I'm going to change the first letter of this word."

"What does this new word say?" Encourage your student to sound out the new word. *Tap*.

Continue to change one letter at a time to form the following words. Each time, have your student sound out the new word.

tap → tan → man → ban → an → at → bat → sat

Lesson 2: Letters N, T, B, and J

New Teaching
(continued)

Complete Activity Sheets

Word Match

Remove page 11 from the *Blast Off* activity book.

Cut out the word cards from the bottom of the page and have your student place the appropriate card under the matching picture.

Ask these questions:

"Which picture starts with the sound /j/?" *Jam.*

"Which picture starts with the sound /m/?" *Man.*

"What is the first sound in the word *bat*?" */b/.*

"What is the first sound in the word *pan*?" */p/.*

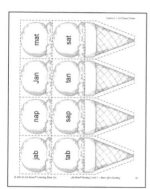

Ice Cream Cones

Remove page 13 from the activity book.

Cut out the ice cream scoops and cones.

Have your student read the words on each ice cream scoop. Put the rhyming words together to form ice cream desserts.

New Teaching
(continued)

The words *an* and *Ann* are homophones (words that sound alike but are spelled differently), as are *mat*, *Matt*, and *matte*. A sentence has been added to the Word Cards *an* and *mat*, and all cards containing homophones in future lessons. Your student does not read these sentences—they are there for your reference in case you wish to discuss the correct word usage.

Practice Reading Words

Have your student practice reading the words on Word Cards 4-12.

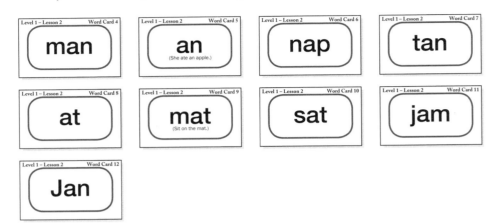

File the Word Cards behind the Review divider of the Reading Review Box.

Teach a Leap Word: *the*

Show Word Card 13 to your student.

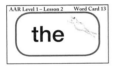

You may wish to explain that we usually pronounce this word as /thŭ/. Sometimes we do say /thē/, but for the purposes of the flashcard review, say the more common pronunciation: /thŭ/.

"Most words follow the rules and say the sounds that we expect them to say. But there are a few words that do not. Here is one of those words."

"This word is *the*, as in *She has the balloons.*"

Point to the frog on the Word Card. "See this frog? This means that the word can't be sounded out. It is a Leap Word that you just need to remember."

"What is this word?" *The.*

Review this Leap Word several times today and then file it behind the Review divider in the Reading Review Box.

Lesson 2: Letters N, T, B, and J

New Teaching
(continued)

Exclamation points are used in the story your student will read in the next lesson.

Practice Fluency

Remove page 15 from the activity book.

Point to a sentence that ends in a period. "This dot is a period. It is used to show the end of the sentence."

Point to a sentence that ends in an exclamation point. "This is an exclamation point. Exclamation points are used to show emotion or excitement."

Model for your student the difference between reading a sentence with a period and reading a sentence with an exclamation point.

Have your student read from the Practice Sheet.

Read-Aloud Time   Read a Story or Poem

Read aloud to your student for twenty minutes.

Track Your Progress   Mark the Progress Chart

Have your student mark Lesson 2 on the Progress Chart.

Lesson 3 - Read "Bam!"

In this lesson, students will read a short story and practice reading sentences with periods and exclamation points.

You will need: ☐ *Blast Off to Reading!* pages 17-19   ☐ Optional: sticky notes
☐ *Run, Bug, Run!* book

Before You Begin

Preview the Story-Related Lessons

You've reached the first story-related lesson in Level 1! Story-related lessons are designed to help your student practice newly learned decoding skills and learn comprehension strategies.

Before reading the story in each story-related lesson, your student will complete several warm-up activities, including a Warm-Up Sheet. The words on the Warm-Up Sheets have been explicitly taught in previous lessons.

You'll notice that there are discussion questions before your student reads the story. The questions are designed to pique your student's interest and activate prior knowledge. The discussions allow your student to relate to the text and attach meaning to what he is about to read.

During and after the story, we ask open-ended questions because we want students to relate to and put thought into what they're reading. We want them to contribute their ideas, test their predictions, and comprehend in a meaningful way. To encourage an active reading process, our reading comprehension strategies also focus on visualizing, questioning, summarizing, making predictions, and drawing conclusions.

Together, these pre- and post-reading activities move your student toward the goal of reading with comprehension.

Post-reading activities include discussing the main character or conflict, story sequencing, imagining alternate endings, and relating the story to your student's life. A complete list of reading comprehension activities can be found in Appendix I.

After completing the warm-up activities in this lesson, your student will read "Bam!" in the *Run, Bug, Run!* book. All the words in the story are decodable using previously taught concepts.

What should you expect when your student reads the stories?
It is normal if your student's reading is choppy at this very early stage. The first time he reads a story, he will probably read just one word at a time. Be patient and encouraging. Subsequent readings will be smoother and more fluent.

Review Word Cards

If you are using *Reading Games with Ziggy the Zebra*, you can play "Ziggy at the Beach" for an engaging way to review Word Cards.

Review

Don't Forget
Always shuffle the Word Cards before reviewing them. By doing so, your student will practice words with a variety of patterns.

Phonogram Cards

Review the Phonogram Cards that are behind the Review divider in your student's Reading Review Box. Show the card to your student and have him say the sound(s). If necessary, remind your student of the sound(s).

Word Cards

Review the Word Cards that are behind the Review divider in your student's Reading Review Box. If your student has difficulty reading the word, build the word with letter tiles and have your student sound it out using the procedure shown in Appendix C: Full Blending Procedure.

New Teaching

This activity will give your student practice with periods and exclamation points, which are used in the upcoming story.

Complete Activity Sheet

"In the last lesson you learned about periods and exclamation points. In this activity, you'll help Rocket the Dog express his excitement with exclamation points."

Down to Earth
Remove pages 17-18 from the *Blast Off* activity book.

Cut out the cards at the top of the sheet.

Tell your student that Rocket the Dog has just landed back on planet Earth and is excited to invite his friends to a picnic. Place a punctuation card (flipped to the "period" side) next to each name and read the names aloud. Then have your student help Rocket the Dog show his excitement by flipping the punctuation cards to reveal the exclamation points.

Read each name again with the exclamation point at the end.

New Teaching
(continued)

Read the Warm-Up Sheet for "Bam!"

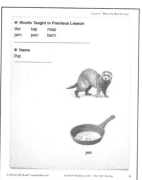

Remove page 19 from the activity book.

Have your student practice reading words and phrases that will be encountered in "Bam!"

Teach Vocabulary and Activate Prior Knowledge

> The purpose of this pre-reading discussion is to introduce new vocabulary that will be used in the story and to activate your student's prior knowledge about curious animals.

Point out the illustration of a ferret on the Warm-Up Sheet. "This is a *ferret*. Ferrets were once used in Europe to catch rats and rabbits, but now they are often kept as pets. Ferrets are quite playful, mischievous, and curious, like cats."

"What are some funny things that cats do? What kind of trouble can they get into?" Discuss your student's experience with and ideas about cats and their behavior.

"Ferrets can get into the same kind of trouble as cats. The story you are about to read is about a curious ferret that gets into a lot of mischief. Let's see what happens!"

Read "Bam!"

> During the story, you will stop your student in several places to model important comprehension strategies. You'll model for your student how to stop to think about unfamiliar words or ideas. You'll also model the beginning stages of making predictions by thinking ahead to what might happen next.
>
> If you wish, you can place a small sticky note at the bottom of pages 13 and 15 of the reader so you remember to stop after reading those pages.

"Turn to page 9 in your reader and read 'Bam!' aloud." Discuss your student's ideas for the questions below as you come to them.

After page 13: "Why do you think the ferret taps the bag?"

After page 15: "What do you think is going to happen to the pan?"

After reading: "What kind of trouble does the ferret get into?" Have your student skim the illustrations for answers.

New Teaching
(continued)

Point Out *The End*

When your student gets to the last page of the story, read the phrase *The End* if your student doesn't already know it. Students generally catch on to this quickly because the phrase is at a predictable part of the story—the end!

Read-Aloud Time

Read a Story or Poem

Read aloud to your student for twenty minutes.

During your read-aloud times, model how you sometimes stop to think about what you are reading. You want your student to understand that good readers think about what they are reading, and that they should expect the text to make sense. Reading is like a conversation between the author and the reader.

Track Your Progress

Mark the Progress Chart

Have your student mark Lesson 3 on the Progress Chart.

Lesson 4 - Letters G, D, C, and Y

This lesson will teach words containing the letters g, d, c, and y, and show that every word has a vowel.

You will need: ☐ Phonogram Cards 9-12   ☐ Word Cards 14-23
☐ Blast Off to Reading! pages 21-25

Before You Begin

The letter y is unusual because it can represent either a consonant sound or a vowel sound.

Y represents a consonant sound in approximately sixty words including *yarn*, *yellow*, and *beyond*. Much more often, in thousands of words, y is a vowel, and it has the same three sounds that i has: /ĭ/–/ī/–/ē/. Y is also part of the vowel teams ay, oy, and ey.

Preview the Sounds of the Letters

Your student will learn the sounds of four letters.

g The letter g can say two sounds:
- /g/ as in *goat*, known as hard g (taught in this lesson)
- /j/ as in *gem*, known as soft g (taught in Lesson 46)

d The letter d says /d/ as in *deer*. Be sure that you and your student don't add /uh/ to the end of the sound, as in /duh/.

c The letter c can say two sounds:
- /k/ as in *cat*, known as hard c (taught in this lesson)
- /s/ as in *city*, known as soft c (taught in Lesson 44)

y The letter y can say four sounds:
- /y/ as in *yarn*, a consonant sound (taught in this lesson)
- /ĭ/ as in *gym*, a vowel sound (taught in Lesson 48)
- /ī/ as in *my*, a vowel sound (taught in Lesson 48)
- /ē/ as in *happy*, a vowel sound (taught in Lesson 48)

In the letter tile demonstrations in this lesson, you will be using the blue y tile to represent the consonant sound of y. In Lesson 48, you will use the red y tile to represent the vowel sounds of y.

Listen to the *Phonogram Sounds* app for a demonstration of the phonogram sounds.

Before You Begin
(continued)

Preview Teaching Every Word Has a Vowel

Your student will learn that every word has a vowel. Later, when multisyllable words are taught, he will learn that every syllable has a vowel. This is helpful to know for decoding longer words.

 If you are using *Reading Games with Ziggy the Zebra*, you can play "Treasure Hunt with Ziggy" for additional practice with this concept.

Review the Practice Sheets

Beginning with this lesson, every Practice Sheet will have a section called "Phrases and Sentences." First there are two short phrases, such as *Jan* and *had a pan*. Then the phrases are combined into a sentence: *Jan had a pan*. This type of practice is called *phrased reading*, and it improves your student's phrasing. Phrasing is important for fluency; fluent readers are able to phrase, or break text into meaningful parts.

If your student does not need practice with phrasing, feel free to skip the first two shorter phrases and have your student read just the full sentence.

How Is Word Card Review Going?

The Word Card review should only take a few minutes each day.

At the beginning of each lesson, choose ten Word Cards from behind the **Review** divider in the Reading Review Box. Shuffle the deck so you are reviewing words that follow different patterns. Keep a Word Card in the review deck until your student can read the word without hesitation.

When it comes time to review mastered Word Cards, choose ten cards or so to review each day. Mix up the cards so your student practices a variety of patterns.

Review

Review the Phonogram Cards that are behind the Review divider in your student's Reading Review Box. Show the card to your student and have him say the sound. If necessary, remind your student of the sound.

Review the Word Cards that are behind the Review divider in your student's Reading Review Box. If your student has difficulty reading the word, build the word with letter tiles and have your student sound it out using the procedure shown in Appendix C: Full Blending Procedure.

New Teaching

Teach New Letter Sounds

Teach the Phonogram Cards for the letters g, d, c, and y.

For each card:
1. Hold up the Phonogram Card and demonstrate the sound.
2. Have your student repeat the sound.
3. Shuffle the new Phonogram Cards and do a mixed review.

File the Phonogram Cards behind the Review divider of the Reading Review Box.

Now practice the same sounds using the letter tiles. Pull these four letter tiles down into your workspace.

Point to each one in random order and ask your student to tell you the sound that each tile makes. Practice until your student can say the sound of each letter accurately.

Practice Commonly Confused Letters

Does your student confuse the letters b and d? If so, see Appendix D for a multisensory solution.

Tip!

Pull down the b and d letter tiles. Randomly dictate /b/ and /d/ to test whether your student can distinguish between the two sounds and choose the correct letter tile.

※ You tube video [b] [d]
The Different Between b and d
by Jack Hartmann

New Teaching
(continued)

Next, pull down the <u>b</u> and <u>p</u> letter tiles. Randomly dictate /b/ and /p/ to see if your student can distinguish between the two sounds and choose the correct letter tile.

If your student has difficulty with either pair of letters, have him watch your mouth as you say the sounds. Review several times, and then add a note to the Review section of the next several lessons so you remember to practice each day.

Blend Sounds with Letter Tiles

Build the word *cab* with letter tiles.

"I'll sound out this first word, and then you'll sound out the next word."

Touch the <u>c</u> and say */k/*.

Touch the <u>a</u> and say */ă/*.

Touch the <u>b</u> and say */b/*.

Now go back to the beginning of the word and blend the sounds together as follows.

Slide your finger under the letters <u>c</u>-<u>a</u> and say */kă/*.

New Teaching
(continued)

> Starting over at the beginning of the word is optional. Some students need the extra support provided by this step, while others do not.
>
> Whenever you feel that your student is ready, blend all three letters without this additional step.

Start at the beginning of the word again. Slide your finger under the letters <u>c</u>-<u>a</u>-<u>b</u> and say *cab* slowly.

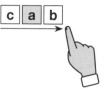

Finally, read the word *cab* at a normal pace, as we do when we speak.

Using the same procedure for blending, have your student sound out the word *mad*.

Play "Change the Word"

Leave the word *mad* on the board. | m | a | d |

"I'm going to change the first letter of this word."

"What does this new word say?" Encourage your student to sound out the new word. *Sad.*

Continue to change one letter at a time to form the following words. Each time, have your student sound out the new word.

sad → pad → pan → can → cap → gap → gas

Teach that Every Word Has a Vowel

"Did you notice that every word we made had a red tile—a vowel?"

Build several words to demonstrate this concept.

New Teaching
(continued)

> The monster can be reused for future practice. Lots of kids like feeding the monster!

Tip!

Complete Activity Sheets

Feed the Monster

Remove pages 21-22 from the *Blast Off* activity book.

Your student can color the monster, if desired. Make a slit in the monster's mouth and cut out the bones.

Have your student read the words on the back of the bones. After reading a word correctly, he should feed the hungry monster by sticking the bone in the monster's mouth.

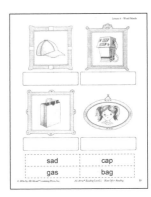

Word Match

Remove page 23 from the activity book.

Cut out the word cards from the bottom of the page and have your student place the appropriate card under the matching picture.

Ask these questions:

"Which picture ends with the sound /g/?" *Bag.*

"Which picture ends with the sound /d/?" *Sad.*

"What is the last sound in the word *gas*?" */s/.*

"What is the last sound in the word *cap*?" */p/.*

Lesson 4: Letters G, D, C, and Y

New Teaching
(continued)

You may need to explain that a yam is a vegetable that tastes like a sweet potato. It grows underground like a regular potato, and it is orange inside.

Practice Reading Words

Have your student practice reading the words on Word Cards 14-23.

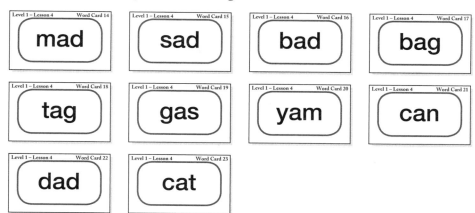

File the Word Cards behind the Review divider of the Reading Review Box.

Practice Fluency

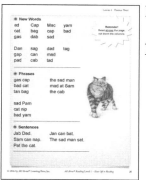

Remove page 25 from the activity book.

Have your student read from the Practice Sheet.

Read-Aloud Time   Read a Story or Poem

Read aloud to your student for twenty minutes.

Track Your Progress

Mark the Progress Chart

Have your student mark Lesson 4 on the Progress Chart.

Lesson 4: Letters G, D, C, and Y

Lesson 5 - Read "The Cat"

In this lesson, students will read a short story and learn words with multiple meanings.

You will need: ☐ *Blast Off to Reading!* pages 27-29

☐ *Run, Bug, Run!* book

Review

Review the Phonogram Cards that are behind the Review divider in your student's Reading Review Box. Show the card to your student and have him say the sound(s). If necessary, remind your student of the sound(s).

Review the Word Cards that are behind the Review divider in your student's Reading Review Box. If your student has difficulty reading the word, build the word with letter tiles and have your student sound it out using the procedure shown in Appendix C: Full Blending Procedure.

New Teaching

Complete Activity Sheet

"Some words can have more than one meaning, like *land*, which can mean *earth* or *to bring a plane to the ground*. In this activity, you'll learn some words with two meanings."

This activity will give your student practice with the words *can* and *tag*, which appear in the upcoming story.

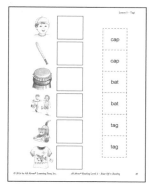

Tag!
Remove page 27 from the *Blast Off* activity book.

Cut out the word cards and lay them face up on the table in front of your student.

Tell your student that you will read some sentences that go with the drawings on the activity sheet. After each sentence, your student should choose the appropriate word card and place it on top of the drawing it matches.

Read the double-meaning word first, and then read the sentence.

New Teaching
(continued)

1. **cap:** This is my favorite baseball cap.
2. **cap:** Will you take the cap off this bottle?
3. **tag:** It is fun to play tag with my friends!
4. **tag:** Please cut this tag off my shirt.
5. **bat:** I hit the ball with a wooden bat.
6. **bat:** My cat likes to bat at balls of yarn.

Read the Warm-Up Sheet for "The Cat"

Remove page 29 from the activity book.

Have your student practice reading words and phrases that will be encountered in "The Cat."

Teach Vocabulary and Activate Prior Knowledge

Point out the illustration of the sun hat on the Warm-Up Sheet. "This is a *sun hat*. A sun hat is often made of straw. Sun hats have a wide, floppy brim to help keep the hot sun off your face. You might wear a sun hat while working in the garden or relaxing at the beach."

"Has anyone or anything ever bothered you while you were trying to relax or sleep? What was it? What did you do about it?" Discuss your student's experiences.

"Sometimes people or even animals can bother us, but they usually don't mean it. In the next story, you'll see how a cat bothers its owner. Let's see what happens!"

New Teaching
(continued)

Read "The Cat"

"Turn to page 19 in your reader and read 'The Cat' aloud." Discuss your student's ideas for the questions below as you come to them.

After page 21: "How does Sam feel about the cat batting the tag? Why does he feel that way?" Have your student look at Sam's expression in the illustration to answer the question.

After page 23: "Does the cat take the hat to be mean? Why or why not?"

After page 24: "How does Sam feel at the end of the story? Do you think he has forgiven the cat? Why?"

Read-Aloud Time

Read a Story or Poem

Read aloud to your student for twenty minutes.

Track Your Progress

Mark the Progress Chart

Have your student mark Lesson 5 on the Progress Chart.

AAAAAAAHHHH!

So you met ... the CAT. Shudder.

Don't let this bubble over my head fool you.
I still get the heebie-jeebies (and the sneezes)
when there's a cat around.

And I know the one in this story personally.
She chased me into a pricker bush once.
Took forever to get the thorns
out of my tail!

No, thank you.
I'll just stay in my nice, safe rocket
until you move on to Lesson 6.

See you on the other side!

Lesson 5: Read "The Cat"

Lesson 6 - Letters H, K, and R

This lesson will teach words containing the letters <u>h</u>, <u>k</u>, and <u>r</u>, as well as the Leap Word <u>a</u>.

You will need: ☐ Phonogram Cards 13-15 ☐ Word Cards 24-32
☐ *Blast Off to Reading!* pages 31-37

Before You Begin

Preview the Sounds of the Letters

Your student will learn the sounds of three letters.

| h | The letter <u>h</u> says /h/ as in *hat*.

| k | The letter <u>k</u> says /k/ as in *kite*.

| r | The letter <u>r</u> says /r/ as in *rake*. A common mistake is to pronounce <u>r</u> as /ruh/. If the sound /r/ is difficult for your student to say in isolation, try having him make a growling noise like a dog: /grrr/. Then say the sound without the initial /g/ sound, leaving just the /rrr/ sound.

Listen to the *Phonogram Sounds* app for a demonstration of the phonogram sounds.

Review Blending

If you are using *Reading Games with Ziggy the Zebra*, you can play "Ziggy Teaches School" whenever your student needs more practice with blending.

Review

Review the Phonogram Cards that are behind the Review divider in your student's Reading Review Box. Show the card to your student and have him say the sound. If necessary, remind your student of the sound.

Don't Forget Choose just ten Word Cards for review each day. Shuffle the cards so your student reviews a variety of patterns.

Review the Word Cards that are behind the Review divider in your student's Reading Review Box. If your student has difficulty reading the word, build the word with letter tiles and have your student sound it out using the procedure shown in Appendix C: Full Blending Procedure.

Ask your student to point to some vowels and some consonants.

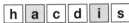

Review the fact that every word has at least one vowel.

New Teaching

Teach New Letter Sounds

Teach the Phonogram Cards for the letters <u>h</u>, <u>k</u>, and <u>r</u>.

For each card:
1. Hold up the Phonogram Card and demonstrate the sound.
2. Have your student repeat the sound.
3. Shuffle the new Phonogram Cards and do a mixed review.

File the Phonogram Cards behind the Review divider of the Reading Review Box.

Now practice the same sounds using the letter tiles. Pull these four letter tiles down into your workspace.

Point to each one in random order and ask your student to tell you the sound that each tile makes. Practice until your student can say the sound of each letter accurately.

New Teaching
(continued)

Blend Sounds with Letter Tiles

Build the word *rat* with letter tiles.

"I'll sound out this first word, and then you'll sound out the next word."

Touch the <u>r</u> and say /*r*/.

Touch the <u>a</u> and say /ă/.

Touch the <u>t</u> and say /*t*/.

Now go back to the beginning of the word and blend the sounds together as follows.

Slide your finger under the letters <u>r</u>-<u>a</u> and say /ră/.

Start at the beginning of the word again. Slide your finger under the letters <u>r</u>-<u>a</u>-<u>t</u> and say *rat* slowly.

Finally, read the word *rat* at a normal pace, as we do when we speak.

Using the same procedure for blending, have your student sound out the word *had*.

h a d

You may wish to make up simple sentences for each new word to give meaning to the word and maintain your student's interest.

Play "Change the Word"

Leave the word *had* on the board.   h a d

"I'm going to change the last letter of this word."

h a → m d

"What does this new word say?" Encourage your student to sound out the new word. *Ham.*

Continue to change one letter at a time to form the following words. Each time, have your student sound out the new word.

ham → hat → rat → mat → mad → had

Complete Activity Sheets

Letter Sounds Bingo

Remove pages 31-33 from the *Blast Off* activity book.

Give your student something fun to use for markers, like raisins, M&Ms, coins, dried beans, or Cheerios.

Randomly call out the sounds of the letters. When a sound is called, your student should put a marker over the corresponding letter. When your student gets three in a row, he says "Bingo!"

For a longer game, have your student fill the card completely before calling bingo.

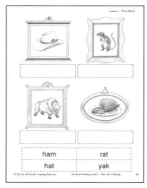

Word Match

Remove page 35 from the activity book.

If necessary, explain that a yak is a large animal with very long, thick hair and horns.

Cut out the word cards from the bottom of the page and have your student place the appropriate card under the matching picture.

New Teaching
(continued)

Ask these questions:

"Which word starts with the sound /y/?" *Yak.*

"Which two words end with the sound /t/?" *Rat and hat.*

"What is the last sound in the word *ham*?" */m/.*

"Which of these are animals?" *Rat and yak.*

"Which is something you can wear?" *Hat.*

"What would look really silly if you put it on your head?" *Rat, yak, or ham.*

Practice Reading Words

Have your student practice reading the words on Word Cards 24-31.

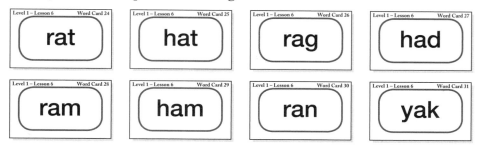

File the Word Cards behind the Review divider of the Reading Review Box.

Teach a Leap Word: *a*

Show Word Card 32 to your student.

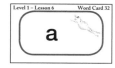

> You may wish to explain that we usually pronounce this word as /ŭ/. Sometimes we do say /ā/, but for the purpose of flashcard review, say the more common pronunciation: /ŭ/.

"Most words follow the rules and say the sounds that we expect them to say. But there are a few words that do not. Here is one of those words."

"This word is *a*, as in *I have a dog.*" Pronounce *a* as /ŭ/, which is the most common pronunciation of this short word.

New Teaching
(continued)

Point to the frog. "This is another Leap Word that you just need to remember."

"What is this word?" *A.*

Review this Leap Word several times today and then file it behind the Review divider in the Reading Review Box.

Don't Forget

Your beginning student isn't expected to read through the entire Practice Sheet in one sitting.

Most students will still be at the stage of sounding out many of the words, and that can be tiring mental work. Stop before your student fatigues. You can always continue during the next class.

Practice Fluency

Remove page 37 from the activity book.

The sentences on this activity sheet end with a period. Remind your student that a period is a punctuation mark used to end a sentence.

Have your student read from the Practice Sheet.

Read-Aloud Time

Read a Story or Poem

Read aloud to your student for twenty minutes.

Track Your Progress

Mark the Progress Chart

Have your student mark Lesson 6 on the Progress Chart.

Lesson 7 - Read "Jam" and "A Hat"

In this lesson, students will read two short stories and "set the table" for one of the stories.

You will need: ☐ *Blast Off to Reading!* pages 39-44

☐ *Run, Bug, Run!* book   ☐ Optional: map or globe

Before You Begin

Preview Lessons with Two Stories

Beginning with this lesson, all story lessons contain two stories. Both stories have Warm-Up Sheets, a vocabulary component, and discussion questions. The first story has an additional component: an activity sheet that is designed to increase your student's comprehension.

Please note that it is fine to stop after the first story and continue the lesson the next day. If the first story is challenging for your student, it may be too much to read a second story. Stop before your student fatigues.

The second story is included for additional practice with the concepts taught in the previous lesson, and the extra reading practice is great for building fluency. If you are working with an advanced student who doesn't need the extra practice, you may choose to skip the second story. (But be forewarned—your student may beg to read those extra stories! There are some fun storylines coming up!)

Review

Don't Forget
Always shuffle the Word Cards before reviewing them. By doing so, your student will practice words with a variety of patterns.

Phonogram Cards

Review the Phonogram Cards that are behind the Review divider in your student's Reading Review Box. Show the card to your student and have him say the sound(s). If necessary, remind your student of the sound(s).

Word Cards

Review the Word Cards that are behind the Review divider in your student's Reading Review Box. If your student has difficulty reading the word, build the word with letter tiles and have your student sound it out using the procedure shown in Appendix C: Full Blending Procedure.

New Teaching

Complete Activity Sheet

"In the story you'll be reading today, a girl has a very unusual dinner guest. Before reading the story, let's help her set the table for two!"

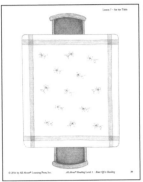

Set the Table

Remove pages 39-41 from the *Blast Off* activity book.

Cut out the table settings cards on page 41.

Have your student arrange them as desired on the illustration of the table. Don't forget the napkins!

Read the Warm-Up Sheet for "Jam"

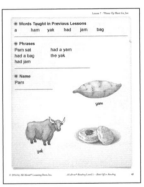

Remove page 43 from the activity book.

Have your student practice reading words and phrases that will be encountered in "Jam."

> **Tip!**
> You will need the flip side of this Warm-Up Sheet for the next story, "A Hat." If you won't be completing that portion of the lesson today, return this Warm-Up Sheet to the activity book for safekeeping.

Teach Vocabulary and Activate Prior Knowledge

Point out the illustration of a yak on the Warm-Up Sheet. "A *yak* is a big, long-haired ox. Yaks can be found in various parts of central Asia."

Point out the illustration of a biscuit on the Warm-Up Sheet. "This is a *biscuit*. A biscuit is a type of small bread roll, often eaten as part of a meal with butter or gravy, or as a sweet treat with jam."

"In this next story, a yak enjoys yams and biscuits at dinner. Have you ever had a friend over for dinner?" Discuss what your student and his friend ate or what they did together.

New Teaching
(continued)

"Have you ever seen a little child get really excited about a food—like ice cream—and that is all she wants to eat?"

"Let's see what happens when the girl in this story serves the yak some jam!"

Read "Jam"

"Turn to page 27 in your reader and read 'Jam' aloud." Discuss your student's ideas for the questions below as you come to them.

After page 31: "What do you think the yak likes most: the ham, the yam, or the jam? Why?" Point out the yak's expression in the illustration.

After page 32: "Do you think Pam is mad that the yak ate all the jam? Why? Do you think she will invite the yak to dinner again?"

Story 2: "A Hat"

Read the Warm-Up Sheet for "A Hat"

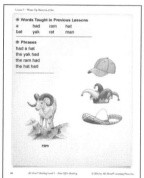

Remove page 44 from the activity book.

Have your student practice reading words and phrases that will be encountered in "A Hat."

Teach Vocabulary and Activate Prior Knowledge

Point out the illustration of a ram on the Warm-Up Sheet. "A *ram* is an adult male sheep. Rams have big horns they use to defend themselves."

Point out the illustration of a sombrero (the hat nearest the bottom of the Warm-Up Sheet). "This is a *sombrero*. A sombrero is a type of hat made of straw. It has a high crown and a very wide brim to protect you from

New Teaching
(continued)

the sun. Sombreros are often worn in Mexico and the southern United States." Point out Mexico on a map or globe.

Point out the illustration of the middle hat on the Warm-Up Sheet. "There are many types of hats. This is a *jester hat*. Jester hats were worn by court jesters, the people that kings and queens used to hire to tell jokes and perform silly acts. What other types of hats can you think of?"

"Have you ever had a really strange dream? What was it about?"

"The girl in the next story has an odd dream about hats. Let's see how it ends."

Read "A Hat"

"Turn to page 37 in your reader and read 'A Hat' aloud." Discuss your student's ideas for the questions below as you come to them.

After page 43: "How do you think this dream will end? Who or what will have a hat next?"

After reading: "Are you surprised at how the story ends? Why?"

Read a Story or Poem

Read aloud to your student for twenty minutes.

Track Your Progress

Mark the Progress Chart

Have your student mark Lesson 7 on the Progress Chart.

Lesson 8 - Letters I, V, F, and Z

This lesson will teach words containing the letters i, v, f, and z.

You will need: ☐ Phonogram Cards 16-19   ☐ Word Cards 33-42

☐ Blast Off to Reading! pages 45-54

Before You Begin

Preview the Sounds of the Letters

Your student will learn the sounds of four letters.

i   The letter i can say three sounds:

- /ĭ/ as in *itchy*, known as the short sound (taught in this lesson)
- /ī/ as in *ivy*, known as the long sound (taught in Lesson 44)
- /ē/ as in *radio* (taught in Lesson 44)

> To help your student remember the sound of short i (/ĭ/), we will use the following hand motion.
>
> **Tip!**
>
> Scratch your forearm with your fingertips as if you are itchy. "When we say /ĭ/, let's pretend that we are itchy. Say the sound of i like this: /ĭ/–/ĭ/–itchy." *Student pretends to have an itch and says /ĭ/–/ĭ/–itchy.*

v   The letter v says /v/ as in *vase*. Be sure that you and your student don't add /uh/ to the end of the sound, as in /vuh/.

f   The letter f says /f/ as in *fish*.

z   The letter z says /z/ as in *zipper*.

   Listen to the *Phonogram Sounds* app for a demonstration of the phonogram sounds.

Before You Begin (continued)	**Preview Word Flippers**

Word Flippers are used in seven lessons and are a fun way to practice fluency. This particular activity requires several minutes of assembly, so you may want to do this before the lesson begins. Refer to Appendix E for instructions.

Review

Review the Phonogram Cards that are behind the Review divider in your student's Reading Review Box. Show the card to your student and have him say the sound(s). If necessary, remind your student of the sound(s).

Review the Word Cards that are behind the Review divider in your student's Reading Review Box. If your student has difficulty reading the word, build the word with letter tiles and have your student sound it out using the procedure shown in Appendix C: Full Blending Procedure.

New Teaching

Teach New Letter Sounds

Hold up the Phonogram Card for the letter i̱.

"This letter says /ĭ/."

Scratch your forearm with your fingertips as if you are itchy. "When we say /ĭ/, let's pretend that we are itchy. Say the sound of i̱ like this: /ĭ/–/ĭ/–itchy." *Student pretends to have an itch and says /ĭ/–/ĭ/–itchy.*

Teach the Phonogram Cards for the letters v̱, f̱, and ẕ.

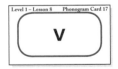 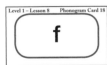 

For each card:
1. Hold up the Phonogram Card and demonstrate the sound.
2. Have your student repeat the sound.
3. Shuffle the new Phonogram Cards and do a mixed review.

File the Phonogram Cards behind the Review divider of the Reading Review Box.

Lesson 8: Letters I, V, F, and Z

New Teaching
(continued)

Now practice the same sounds using the letter tiles. Pull these four letter tiles down into your workspace.

Point to each one in random order and ask your student to tell you the sound that each tile makes. Practice until your student can say the sound of each letter accurately.

Blend Sounds with Letter Tiles

Build the word *dip* with letter tiles.   d i p

"I'll sound out this first word, and then you'll sound out the next word."

Touch the <u>d</u> and say /d/.

Touch the <u>i</u> and say /ĭ/.

Touch the <u>p</u> and say /p/.

Now go back to the beginning of the word and blend the sounds together as follows.

Slide your finger under the letters <u>d</u>-<u>i</u> and say /dĭ/.

Start at the beginning of the word again. Slide your finger under the letters <u>d</u>-<u>i</u>-<u>p</u> and say *dip* slowly.

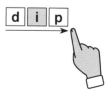

Don't Forget

Starting over at the beginning of the word is optional. Some students need the extra support provided by this step, while others do not.

Whenever you feel that your student is ready, blend all three letters without this additional step.

New Teaching
(continued)

Finally, read the word *dip* at a normal pace, as we do when we speak.

Using the same procedure for blending, have your student sound out the word *fan*.

Play "Change the Word"

Build the word *him*. | h | i | m |

"What is this word?" *Him.*

"I'm going to change the last letter of this word."

"What does this new word say?" Encourage your student to sound out the new word. *Hit.*

Continue to change one letter at a time to form the following words. Each time, have your student sound out the new word.

**hit → sit → pit → bit → fit → fig →
big → bid → hid → rid → rip**

Complete Activity Sheet

Word Flippers for Short Vowel Sounds
Remove pages 45-51 from the *Blast Off* activity book.

Refer to Appendix E for assembly instructions.

Have your student turn the pages and read the words that are formed.

Tip!

If the vowels cause difficulty, have your student point to the vowel and say the sound of the vowel before starting to sound out the word. For example, with the word *bit*, your student would point to the vowel and say /ĭ/, and then sound out the word from the beginning.

Use this tip whenever your student has difficulty with vowels.

Lesson 8: Letters I, V, F, and Z

New Teaching
(continued)

Practice Reading Words

Have your student practice reading the words on Word Cards 33-42.

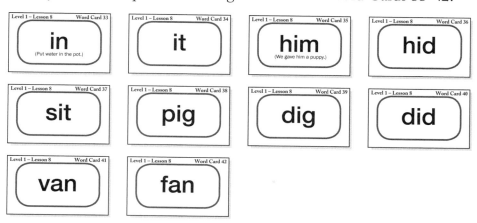

File the Word Cards behind the Review divider of the Reading Review Box.

Practice Fluency

> Question marks and commas are used in the stories your student will read in the next lesson.

Remove pages 53-54 from the activity book.

Point to a sentence that ends in a question mark. "This is a question mark. It is used to show that the sentence is a question, like *How are you?*"

Model for your student the difference between reading a sentence with a period and reading a sentence with a question mark.

Point to a sentence that contains a comma. "This is a comma. Commas are used to indicate a short pause. We generally don't pause as long for a comma as we do for a period."

Model for your student how to read sentences with a comma.

Have your student read from the Practice Sheet.

New Teaching
(continued)

Don't Forget Today's Practice Sheet is two pages long, and you'll need to be the judge of whether your student needs all of this practice.

For older learners needing remedial work, this extra practice is critical to their success. For younger learners whose eye muscles are still developing, you should choose a reasonable number of lines to practice. Every situation is different, and you need to do what is best for your student.

Read-Aloud Time

Read a Story or Poem

Read aloud to your student for twenty minutes.

Track Your Progress

Mark the Progress Chart

Have your student mark Lesson 8 on the Progress Chart.

Lesson 8: Letters I, V, F, and Z

Lesson 9 - Read "Hit the Gas" and "The Bad Rat"

In this lesson, students will read two short stories and practice punctuation marks.

You will need: ☐ *Blast Off to Reading!* pages 55-58

☐ *Run, Bug, Run!* book

Review

Shuffle and review the cards behind the Review dividers daily. Doing so gives your student practice with a variety of concepts presented in random order.

Don't Forget

Review the Phonogram Cards that are behind the Review divider in your student's Reading Review Box. Show the card to your student and have him say the sound(s). If necessary, remind your student of the sound(s).

Review the Word Cards that are behind the Review divider in your student's Reading Review Box. If your student has difficulty reading the word, build the word with letter tiles and have your student sound it out using the procedure shown in Appendix C: Full Blending Procedure.

New Teaching

Story 1: "Hit the Gas"

Complete Activity Sheet

The story "Hit the Gas" uses the question mark, which was introduced in Lesson 8. Before beginning this activity sheet, review the terms *period, exclamation point,* and *question mark* with your student.

"You have learned about periods, exclamation points, and question marks. In this activity, you'll practice using each punctuation mark."

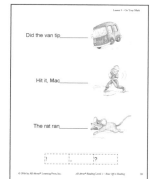

On Your Mark

Remove page 55 from the *Blast Off* activity book.

Cut out the punctuation mark cards on the bottom of the page and lay them face up on the table.

Have your student read each sentence and then decide which punctuation mark should be used at the end. Once he's decided, he should place the punctuation card in the space provided. You may help your student choose the correct punctuation mark by discussing the sentences.

New Teaching
(continued)

Don't Forget

You will need the flip side of this Warm-Up Sheet for the next story, "The Bad Rat." If you won't be completing that portion of the lesson today, return this Warm-Up Sheet to the activity book for safekeeping.

Read the Warm-Up Sheet for "Hit the Gas"

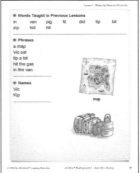

Remove page 57 from the activity book.

Have your student practice reading words and phrases that will be encountered in "Hit the Gas."

Point out the name *Vic* in the Names section of the Warm-Up Sheet. "In the next story, the girl is named Vic. Vic is short for Victoria. When we shorten a person's name or call her by a different name, we call it a *nickname*. Do you or does someone you know have a nickname?"

Teach Vocabulary and Activate Prior Knowledge

Point out the illustration of luggage on the Warm-Up Sheet. "This is *luggage.* Luggage is all the bags, suitcases, and other items that you take with you when you go on a trip."

"Have you ever gone on a trip in a car? Where did you put the luggage?" Discuss where your student went or what he saw on the trip.

"If you could take a trip anywhere, where would you go?"

Turn to page 47 in the reader and point out the title of the story. "If I tell the driver of a car to 'hit the gas,' do I mean to go or to stop? What if I say 'hit the brakes'?"

"In this story, a girl goes on a trip with a lot of unusual friends. Let's see what happens."

Read "Hit the Gas"

"Turn to page 47 in your reader and read 'Hit the Gas' aloud." Discuss your student's ideas for the questions below as you come to them.

After page 49: "Look at the illustration. What items is Vic bringing with her?" *Plant, doghouse, food bowl, suitcase, pig feed, apples, cheese.*

"Based on those items, what kind of friends do you think will go on the trip with Vic?"

After page 54: "Where do you think Vic and the animals are going?"

Lesson 9: Read "Hit the Gas" and "The Bad Rat"

New Teaching
(continued)

Don't Forget

The remaining story lessons contain two stories to read. If you see that your student is fatigued after reading the first story, you may wish to split the lesson in two and read the second story the next day.

Read the Warm-Up Sheet for "The Bad Rat"

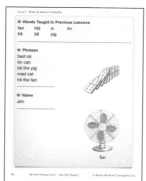

Remove page 58 from the activity book.

Have your student practice reading words and phrases that will be encountered in "The Bad Rat."

Teach Vocabulary and Activate Prior Knowledge

Point out the illustration of the toppling dominoes on the Warm-Up Sheet. "These are dominoes. If you set up dominoes like this and knock over the first one, that domino will knock over the second domino, the second domino will knock over the third domino, and so on until all the dominoes fall down. This is called a *chain reaction*. A chain reaction is when one event leads to another event, and so on and so on."

"In this next story, a bad rat sets off a chain reaction."

"Have you ever seen an animal make a mess or break something? How did the animal act afterwards?" Discuss your student's experience.

"Let's see what the bad rat in this story does."

Read "The Bad Rat"

"Turn to page 57 in your reader and read 'The Bad Rat' aloud." Discuss your student's ideas for the questions below as you come to them.

After page 60: "Why do you think the pig bites the cat?"

After page 64: "Do you think the rat will bite anyone anymore? Why?"

Read-Aloud Time   Read a Story or Poem

Read aloud to your student for twenty minutes.

Track Your Progress

Mark the Progress Chart

Have your student mark Lesson 9 on the Progress Chart.

M, A, B, J, Y,
O, C, K, Z, F ...

Whew!
All those letters warped my woofer
for a while, but now I have them all straight.
And you're doing great, too!

Keep it up, fellow space dog!

Lesson 9: Read "Hit the Gas" and "The Bad Rat"

Lesson 10 - Letters O, L, and W

This lesson will teach words containing the letters o, l, and w, as well as the Leap Word of.

You will need: ☐ Phonogram Cards 20-22   ☐ Word Cards 43-52
☐ Blast Off to Reading! pages 59-62

Before You Begin

Preview the Sounds of the Letters

Your student will learn the sounds of three letters.

o The letter o can say four sounds:

- /ŏ/ as in *otter*, known as the short sound (taught in this lesson)
- /ō/ as in *open*, known as the long sound (taught in Lesson 46)
- /ōō/ as in *to* (taught in Lesson 46)
- /ŭ/ as in *oven* (taught in Lesson 46)

To help your student remember the sound of short o (/ŏ/), we will use the following hand motion. **Tip!**

Form an "o" shape with one hand and hold it to your nose. "When we say /ŏ/, let's pretend that we have a nose like an otter. Say the sound of o like this: /ŏ/–/ŏ/–otter." *Student makes an otter nose and says /ŏ/–/ŏ/–otter.*

l The letter l says /l/ as in *leaf*. Be sure that you and your student don't add /uh/ to the end of the sound, as in /luh/.

w The letter w says /w/ as in *wave*. It is impossible to say /w/ in isolation without any trace of /uh/ at the end, but clip the /uh/ as short as possible.

Listen to the *Phonogram Sounds* app for a demonstration of the phonogram sounds.

Review

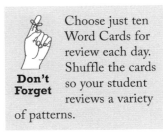
Choose just ten Word Cards for review each day. Shuffle the cards so your student reviews a variety of patterns.

Don't Forget

Review the Phonogram Cards that are behind the Review divider in your student's Reading Review Box. Show the card to your student and have him say the sound. If necessary, remind your student of the sound.

Review the Word Cards that are behind the Review divider in your student's Reading Review Box. If your student has difficulty reading the word, build the word with letter tiles and have your student sound it out using the procedure shown in Appendix C: Full Blending Procedure.

New Teaching

Teach New Letter Sounds

Hold up the Phonogram Card for the letter o.

"This letter says /ŏ/."

Form an "o" shape with one hand and hold it to your nose. "When we say /ŏ/, let's pretend that we have a nose like an otter. Say the sound of o like this: /ŏ/–/ŏ/–otter." *Student makes an otter nose and says /ŏ/–/ŏ/–otter.*

Teach the Phonogram Cards for the letters l and w.

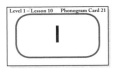 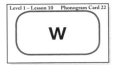

For each card:
1. Hold up the Phonogram Card and demonstrate the sound.
2. Have your student repeat the sound.
3. Shuffle the new Phonogram Cards and do a mixed review.

Now practice the same sounds using the letter tiles. Pull these three letter tiles down into your workspace.

Point to each one in random order and ask your student to tell you the sound that each tile makes. Practice until your student can say the sound of each letter accurately.

New Teaching
(continued)

Blend Sounds with Letter Tiles

Build the word *lid* with letter tiles.

"I'll sound out this first word, and then you'll sound out the next word."

Touch the l and say /l/.

Touch the i and say /ĭ/.

Touch the d and say /d/.

Now go back to the beginning of the word and blend the sounds together as follows.

Slide your finger under the letters l-i and say /lĭ/.

This is the last lesson in which we start at the beginning of the word for a second time. If you feel that your student still needs this step, feel free to add it in.

Start at the beginning of the word again. Slide your finger under the letters l-i-d and say *lid* slowly.

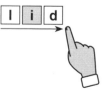

Finally, read the word *lid* at a normal pace, as we do when we speak.

Using the same procedure for blending, have your student sound out the word *wig*.

| w | i | g |

Lesson 10: Letters o, l, and w

New Teaching
(continued)

Play "Change the Word"

Build the word *sob*.

"What is this word?" *Sob.*

"I'm going to change the first letter of this word."

```
  m
  ↓   o  b
  s
```

"What does this new word say?" Encourage your student to sound out the new word. *Mob.*

Continue to change one letter at a time to form the following words. Each time, have your student sound out the new word.

**mob → mop → top → hop → hot →
rot → pot → got**

Complete Activity Sheet

Word Match

Remove page 59 from the *Blast Off* activity book.

Cut out the word cards from the bottom of the page and have your student place the appropriate card under the matching picture.

Ask these questions:

"Which word starts with the sound /m/?" *Mop.*

"Which two words end with the sound /g/?" *Dog and log.*

New Teaching
(continued)

Don't Forget

Remember: if the vowels cause difficulty, have your student point to the vowel and say its sound before beginning to sound out the word. For example, with the word *job*, your student would point to the vowel and say /ŏ/, and then sound out the word from the beginning.

Practice Reading Words

Have your student practice reading the words on Word Cards 43-51.

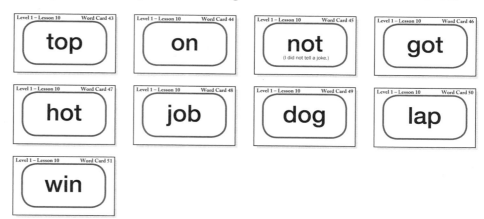

File the Word Cards behind the Review divider of the Reading Review Box.

Teach a Leap Word: *of*

The word *of* is the only word in which the letter f says /v/.

Show Word Card 52 to your student.

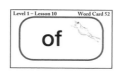

"Most words follow the rules and say the sounds that we expect them to say. But there are a few words that do not. Here is one of those words."

"This word is *of*, as in *Let's get more of those fish.*"

"The o and the f don't say the sounds we expect them to say, so this is a Leap Word."

Review this Leap Word several times today and then file it behind the Review divider in the Reading Review Box.

New Teaching
(continued)

Quotation marks and ellipses are used in the stories your student will read in the next lesson.

Practice Fluency

Remove pages 61-62 from the activity book.

Point to the sentence that contains quotation marks. "These are quotation marks. They are used to show that someone is speaking. Notice how they are placed at the beginning and the end of the sentence being spoken."

Point to the sentence that contains an ellipsis. "When you see three dots like this, it means there is a big pause in the sentence, or the sentence is not finished. These dots can be used in the middle or at the end of a sentence."

Model for your student how to read sentences with quotation marks and ellipses.

Have your student read from the Practice Sheet.

Read-Aloud Time

Read a Story or Poem

Read aloud to your student for twenty minutes.

Track Your Progress

Mark the Progress Chart

Have your student mark Lesson 10 on the Progress Chart.

Lesson 10: Letters o, l, and w

Lesson 11 - Read "Jan Did It" and "The Job"

In this lesson, students will read two short stories and create a chore chart.

You will need: ☐ *Blast Off to Reading!* pages 63-68

☐ *Run, Bug, Run!* book   ☐ Optional: video of an Irish jig

Review

 How is the daily review going? Are the decks behind the **Mastered** dividers getting bigger?

Mastered cards will be reviewed in Step 11 to keep them fresh in your student's mind.

 Review the Phonogram Cards that are behind the Review divider in your student's Reading Review Box. Show the card to your student and have him say the sound(s). If necessary, remind your student of the sound(s).

 Review the Word Cards that are behind the Review divider in your student's Reading Review Box. If your student has difficulty reading the word, build the word with letter tiles and have your student sound it out using the procedure shown in Appendix C: Full Blending Procedure.

New Teaching

Story 1: "Jan Did It"

Complete Activity Sheet

"Do you have any small jobs to do around the house? What are they?"

"In this activity, you'll make your own chore chart."

Chore Chart
Remove pages 63-65 from the *Blast Off* activity book.

Cut out the chore cards on page 65.

Have your student create her own visual chore chart by attaching the chore cards to the "Jobs" list on page 63. If your student has special chores not represented in the illustrations, she may draw them on the blank chore cards provided and add them to the jobs list.

New Teaching
(continued)

Don't Forget

You will need the flip side of this Warm-Up Sheet for the next story, "The Job." If you won't be completing that portion of the lesson today, return this Warm-Up Sheet to the activity book for safekeeping.

Show video of "dance a jig"

Read the Warm-Up Sheet for "Jan Did It"

Remove page 67 from the activity book.

Have your student practice reading words and phrases that will be encountered in "Jan Did It."

Teach Vocabulary and Activate Prior Knowledge

Point out the illustration of a jig on the Warm-Up Sheet. "A *jig* is an energetic dance. If someone dances a jig, you will see them hopping or skipping to the music. A common type of jig is an Irish jig." Locate a YouTube video of an Irish jig and show it to your student.

"The girl in this story is very busy. Let's see what she has on her list of things to do."

Read "Jan Did It"

"Turn to page 67 in your reader and read 'Jan Did It' aloud." Discuss your student's ideas for the questions below as you come to them.

After page 68: "What jobs are on Jan's list of things to do?"

> You may need to explain these words to your student: *jog* (slow run) and *sob* (cry).

After page 74: "Why do you think Jan did not sob?"

Lesson 11: Read "Jan Did It" and "The Job"

New Teaching
(continued)

Read the Warm-Up Sheet for "The Job"

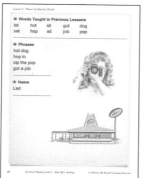

Remove page 68 from the activity book.

Have your student practice reading words and phrases that will be encountered in "The Job."

Teach Vocabulary and Activate Prior Knowledge

Point out the illustration of a drive-in restaurant on the Warm-Up Sheet. "This is a *drive-in restaurant*. At this type of restaurant, you stay in your car. A waiter comes out to take your order and then delivers your meal to your car. Sometimes they have special trays you can attach to your car door."

"Our next story takes place in a drive-in restaurant. The place where a story happens is called the *setting*."

Point out the illustration of the photographer on the Warm-Up Sheet. "This is a *photographer*. Photographers take pictures for a living. They work for magazines, newspapers, advertising agencies, and many other types of companies."

"Have you ever had your picture taken with a camera?" Discuss when and where your student had his picture taken.

"In this story, someone takes a picture of a dog and makes him famous! Let's see how that happens."

New Teaching
(continued)

Read "The Job"

"Turn to page 77 in your reader and read 'The Job' aloud." Discuss your student's ideas for the questions below as you come to them.

After page 79: "What kind of job do you think Lad has?"

After page 86: "Look at the illustration. What is Lad's ad for?"

Read-Aloud Time

Read a Story or Poem

Read aloud to your student for twenty minutes.

Track Your Progress

Mark the Progress Chart

Have your student mark Lesson 11 on the Progress Chart.

Lesson 12 - Letter U and the Second Sound of S

This lesson will teach words containing the letter u and the second sound of s.

You will need: ☐ Phonogram Cards 2 and 23   ☐ Word Cards 53-62
☐ Blast Off to Reading! pages 69-74

Before You Begin

Preview the Sounds of the Letters

Your student will learn the sounds of u and the second sound of s.

u   The letter u can say three sounds:

- /ŭ/ as in *udder*, known as the short sound (taught in this lesson)
- /ū/ as in *unit*, known as the long sound (taught in Lesson 48)
- /ŏŏ/ as in *put* (taught in Lesson 48)

> To help your student remember the sound of short u (/ŭ/), we will use the following hand motion.   **Tip!**
>
> Using both hands, do a hand motion like you are milking a cow. "When we say /ŭ/, let's pretend that we are farmers milking a cow. Say the sound of u like this: /ŭ/–/ŭ/–udder." *Student pretends to milk a cow and says /ŭ/–/ŭ/–udder.*

s   Your student has already learned that s says /s/. In this lesson, we will add the second sound of s: /z/ as in *has*.

   Listen to the *Phonogram Sounds* app for a demonstration of the phonogram sounds.

Preview More Information on S

When it occurs at the beginning of a word, s says /s/ as in *sun*. When it occurs at the end of the word, sometimes it says /s/ and sometimes it says /z/. In this lesson, students will learn that they should try the first sound, /s/, and if that doesn't sound like a real word, try the second sound.

There are some guidelines to figure out whether final s will say /s/ or /z/, but it involves much more mental work than simply trying the /s/ sound first. We won't be teaching these guidelines to your student, but for your information, here is the pattern:

- If the preceding sound is /f/, /k/, /p/, or /t/, final s usually says /s/.
  cliffs   sticks   lips   acts   paths

- If the preceding sound is /b/, /d/, /g/, /l/, /m/, /n/, /ng/, /r/, or /v/, final s usually says /z/.
  **tabs   lids   logs   hills   moms
  hens   cars   lives   wings**

- If the preceding sound is a vowel sound, final s may say /s/ or /z/.
  gas   has

It's much simpler and more effective to have the student try the first sound of s, and if that doesn't produce a real word, then try the second sound.

Freeing Up Mental Space for Comprehension

Reading requires two main tasks:
1. Fluently decoding the printed word
2. Comprehending the printed word

For beginning readers, decoding is very difficult because they have to work so hard to sound out words to pronounce them. This takes up so much of a beginning reader's attention that your student's mind actually switches between decoding and comprehending a few words at a time. That's why a student's reading can be somewhat choppy when he is initially learning to read. It's all a part of the process!

By consistently working through the fluency exercises, though, your student will learn to decode the printed word more quickly and easily, which will free up the mental space and attention needed for reading comprehension.

Review

Don't Forget

Choose just ten Word Cards for review each day. Shuffle the cards so your student reviews a variety of patterns.

Review the Phonogram Cards that are behind the Review divider in your student's Reading Review Box. Show the card to your student and have him say the sound. If necessary, remind your student of the sound.

Review the Word Cards that are behind the Review divider in your student's Reading Review Box. If your student has difficulty reading the word, build the word with letter tiles and have your student sound it out using the procedure shown in Appendix C: Full Blending Procedure.

New Teaching

Don't Forget

Whenever you introduce a new Phonogram Card, remember to file it behind the appropriate **Review** divider in your student's Reading Review Box.

Even if your student appears to remember the new phonogram during his first introduction to it, you'll want to revisit it during your next lesson. You want to make sure that the Phonogram Card has really been mastered before moving it behind the **Mastered** divider.

Teach New Letter Sounds

Hold up the Phonogram Card for the letter <u>u</u>.

"This letter says /ŭ/."

Using both hands, do a hand motion like you are milking a cow. "When we say /ŭ/, let's pretend that we are farmers milking a cow. Say the sound of <u>u</u> like this: /ŭ/–/ŭ/–udder." *Student pretends to milk a cow and says /ŭ/–/ŭ/–udder.*

Take out Phonogram Card 2 and show it to your student.

"You already know that the letter <u>s</u> says /s/. But it also makes another sound: /z/. So the letter <u>s</u> makes two sounds: /s/ and /z/. Repeat after me: /s/–/z/." *Student repeats.*

File the Phonogram Cards behind the Review divider of the Reading Review Box.

Build the words *us* and *is* with letter tiles. | u | s | | i | s |

"When the letter <u>s</u> is at the end of a word, sometimes it says its first sound and sometimes it says its second sound. Try the first sound, and if that doesn't sound like a real word, try the second sound."

Practice this concept with the words *us* and *is*.

Blend Sounds with Letter Tiles

Build the word *hut* with letter tiles.

"I'll sound out this first word, and then you'll sound out the next word."

Touch the <u>h</u> and say /h/.

Touch the <u>u</u> and say /ŭ/.

Touch the <u>t</u> and say /t/.

Now go back to the beginning of the word. Slide your finger under the letters <u>h</u>-<u>u</u>-<u>t</u> and say *hut* slowly.

Finally, read the word *hut* at a normal pace, as we do when we speak.

Using the same procedure for blending, have your student sound out the word *rub*.

New Teaching
(continued)

Play "Change the Word"

Build the word *hum*. h u m

"What is this word?" *Hum.*

"I'm going to change the first letter of this word."

g
↓
h   u m

"What does this new word say?" Encourage your student to sound out the new word. *Gum.*

Continue to change one letter at a time to form the following words. Each time, have your student sound out the new word.

**gum → gun → bun → sun → run → rub → rug →
dug → tug → bug**

This next sequence contains the second sound of <u>s</u>. Change one letter at a time to form the following words.

is → his → has → as

Complete Activity Sheet

Letter Sounds Bingo
Remove pages 69-71 from the *Blast Off* activity book.

Give your student something fun to use for markers, like raisins, M&Ms, coins, dried beans, or Cheerios.

Randomly call out the sounds of the letters. When a sound is called, your student should put a marker over the corresponding letter. When your student gets three in a row, he says "Bingo!"

For a longer game, have your student fill the card completely before calling bingo.

Practice Reading Words

Have your student practice reading the words on Word Cards 53-62.

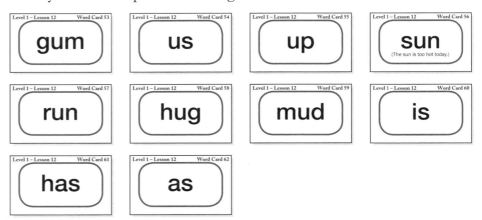

File the Word Cards behind the Review divider of the Reading Review Box.

Practice Fluency

Remove pages 73-74 from the activity book.

Have your student read from the Practice Sheet.

Read-Aloud Time ## Read a Story or Poem

Read aloud to your student for twenty minutes.

Lesson 12: Letter U and the Second Sound of S

Track Your Progress

Mark the Progress Chart

Have your student mark Lesson 12 on the Progress Chart.

Can you believe we've
been through twelve lessons already?
We are STELLAR!

And we've read a whole galaxy of stories, too.
Did you see that dog in "The Job"?
Sure, he has cute spots and all, but I think
I would have been amazing
in that hotdog ad!

Who wouldn't like
gravity-defying hotdogs?

Lesson 12: Letter U and the Second Sound of S

Lesson 13 - Read "Run, Bug, Run!" and "Kip the Pup"

In this lesson, students will read two short stories and imagine life from the viewpoint of a character.

You will need: ☐ *Blast Off to Reading!* pages 75-78

☐ *Run, Bug, Run!* book

Review

Review the Phonogram Cards that are behind the Review divider in your student's Reading Review Box. Show the card to your student and have him say the sound(s). If necessary, remind your student of the sound(s).

Review the Word Cards that are behind the Review divider in your student's Reading Review Box. If your student has difficulty reading the word, build the word with letter tiles and have your student sound it out using the procedure shown in Appendix C: Full Blending Procedure.

Shuffle the cards behind the **Mastered** dividers and choose a random selection of 10-20 cards for review.

New Teaching

Story 1: "Run, Bug, Run!"

Complete Activity Sheet

"Imagine how scary the world would be if you were as small as a bug. In this activity, you'll help a bug stay out of danger."

Is It Dangerous?
Remove page 75 from the *Blast Off* activity book.

Cut out the cards and set aside the bug card. Mix up the remaining seven cards and place them face down in a pile. Have your student select the cards one by one and decide whether the object pictured would be dangerous to the bug or if it's safe. If desired, your student may make separate piles for dangerous and safe objects.

New Teaching
(continued)

Don't Forget

You will need the flip side of this Warm-Up Sheet for the next story, "Kip the Pup." If you won't be completing that portion of the lesson today, return this Warm-Up Sheet to the activity book for safekeeping.

Read the Warm-Up Sheet for "Run, Bug, Run!"

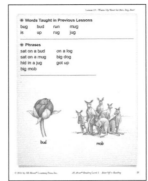

Remove page 77 from the activity book.

Have your student practice reading words and phrases that will be encountered in "Run, Bug, Run!"

Teach Vocabulary and Activate Prior Knowledge

Point out the illustration of a bud on the Warm-Up Sheet. "A *bud* is a new leaf or flower that is still closed and that is getting ready to open. There is a rose bud in today's story. That means a new rose that is just beginning to open its petals."

Point out the illustration of a mob on the Warm-Up Sheet. "A *mob* is a large group. A group of cows is called a *herd*. A group of dogs is called a *pack*. And a group of kangaroos is called a *mob*."

"The word *mob* can actually refer to any large group. For example, if there was a mob of mosquitoes outside last night, that means there were lots and lots of mosquitoes. In this next story, the main character is an insect. At first he is alone, but then he finds a mob."

"What is the opposite of a mob?" Possible answers: *one or two, a small number.*

"If you were as small as a bug, where would you hide to stay safe?" Discuss various places a small bug could hide.

"Let's see what the little bug in this story does to stay out of danger."

　Lesson 13: Read "Run, Bug, Run!" and "Kip the Pup"

New Teaching
(continued)

Read "Run, Bug, Run!"

"Turn to page 89 in your reader and read 'Run, Bug, Run!' aloud." Discuss your student's ideas for the questions below as you come to them.

After page 96: "Why isn't the bug afraid of the big mob?"

After reading: "Go back to the beginning of the story and look at the illustrations. What danger is the bug in on each page?"

Story 2: "Kip the Pup"

Read the Warm-Up Sheet for "Kip the Pup"

Remove page 78 from the activity book.

Have your student practice reading words and phrases that will be encountered in "Kip the Pup."

Teach Vocabulary and Activate Prior Knowledge

Point out the illustration of a hut on the Warm-Up Sheet. "A *hut* is a type of shelter. It is usually small, and it can be made from a variety of different things. The one in this illustration is made of stone and straw. Huts can also be made of sticks, mud, or wood. An igloo is a type of hut that is made of snow and ice."

"Have you ever seen a puppy playing outside? What kinds of things do puppies like to do?" Discuss ways that puppies have fun.

"In this next story, a pup has all sorts of fun. And he even has a hut!"

New Teaching
(continued)

Read "Kip the Pup"

"Turn to page 99 in your reader and read 'Kip the Pup' aloud." Discuss your student's ideas for the questions below as you come to them.

After reading: "Kip does two things that are a bit naughty. What are these two things?" *Biting the hose/sprinkler and digging up the flowers.*

"Why do you think Kip doesn't get in trouble for being naughty?"

Read-Aloud Time

Read a Story or Poem

Read aloud to your student for twenty minutes.

Track Your Progress

Mark the Progress Chart

Have your student mark Lesson 13 on the Progress Chart.

Lesson 14 - Letter E

This lesson will teach words containing the letter *e*.

You will need: ☐ Phonogram Card 24   ☐ Word Cards 63-72

☐ *Blast Off to Reading!* pages 79-84

Before You Begin

Preview the Sounds of the Letter

| e | The letter *e* can say two sounds:

- /ĕ/ as in *echo*, known as the short sound (taught in this lesson)
- /ē/ as in *even*, known as the long sound (taught in Lesson 48)

To help your student remember the sound of short *e* (/ĕ/), we will use the following hand motion. **Tip!**

Cup your hand to your ear as if you are listening to an echo. "When we say /ĕ/, let's pretend that we are listening to an echo. Say the sound of *e* like this: /ĕ/–/ĕ/–echo." *Student pretends to listen for an echo and says /ĕ/–/ĕ/–echo.*

 Listen to the *Phonogram Sounds* app for a demonstration of the phonogram sounds.

Preview Function Words

Function words are short words like *the, at, an, can, am, a, if, of,* and *is*. Function words can't be described (What does *if* mean?), and they are normally unstressed (*I'kn ride'uh bike* instead of *I can ride a bike*)—yet they are the glue that holds our sentences together.

Function words make up a high percentage of our reading material, but some beginning readers need extra time to learn them. To give your student extra practice with function words, they have been sprinkled throughout the Practice Sheets.

<table>
<tr>
<td>

Before You Begin
(continued)

</td>
<td>

A Tip Regarding Vowels I and E

Some students have difficulty with words containing short i and short e, which sound similar to untrained ears. If your student says the wrong sound, ask him to first touch the vowel and say the vowel sound with its related mnemonic (/ĕ/ –/ĕ/ –echo or /ĭ/ –/ĭ/ –itchy). Then he should go back and sound out the word from the beginning.

</td>
</tr>
</table>

Review

Review the Phonogram Cards that are behind the Review divider in your student's Reading Review Box. Show the card to your student and have him say the sound. If necessary, remind your student of the sound.

Review the Word Cards that are behind the Review divider in your student's Reading Review Box. If your student has difficulty reading the word, build the word with letter tiles and have your student sound it out using the procedure shown in Appendix C: Full Blending Procedure.

New Teaching

Teach New Letter Sounds

Hold up the Phonogram Card for the letter e.

"This letter says /ĕ/."

Cup your hand to your ear as if you are listening to an echo. "When we say /ĕ/, let's pretend that we are listening to an echo. Say the sound of e like this: /ĕ/ –/ĕ/ –echo." *Student pretends to listen for an echo and says /ĕ/ –/ĕ/ –echo.*

Mix in several other Phonogram Cards for mixed review and practice until your student can say the sounds accurately. File the new Phonogram Card behind the Review divider in the Reading Review Box.

Set out the new letter tile.

Mix in several other letter tiles for mixed review and practice with the new tile until your student can say the sounds accurately.

New Teaching
(continued)

Blend Sounds with Letter Tiles

Build the word *bed* with letter tiles.   b e d

"I'll sound out this first word, and then you'll sound out the next word."

Touch the b and say /b/.

Touch the e and say /ĕ/.

Touch the d and say /d/.

Now go back to the beginning of the word. Slide your finger under the letters b-e-d and say *bed* slowly.

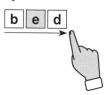

Finally, read the word *bed* at a normal pace, as we do when we speak.

Using the same procedure for blending, have your student sound out the word *set*.

s e t

Play "Change the Word"

Build the word *jet*.

"What is this word?" *Jet.*

"I'm going to change the first letter of this word."

"What does this new word say?" Encourage your student to sound out the new word. *Met.*

Continue to change one letter at a time to form the following words. Each time, have your student sound out the new word.

met → men → hen → pen → pet → bet → yet → yes

Complete Activity Sheet

Monkeys and Bananas

Remove pages 79-82 from the *Blast Off* activity book.

Have your student choose a monkey and read the monkey's name.

Your student should find the bananas that rhyme with the monkey's name and read each of the rhyming words.

Your student can then choose a new monkey and repeat the exercise.

Practice Reading Words

Have your student practice reading the words on Word Cards 63-72.

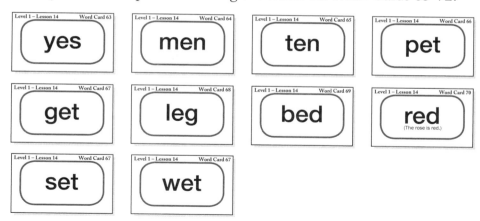

File the Word Cards behind the Review divider of the Reading Review Box.

Practice Fluency

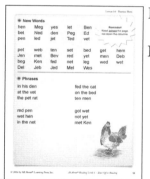

Remove pages 83-84 from the activity book.

Have your student read from the Practice Sheet.

Read-Aloud Time   Read a Story or Poem

Read aloud to your student for twenty minutes.

Track Your Progress

Mark the Progress Chart

Have your student mark Lesson 14 on the Progress Chart.

Lesson 15 - Read "The Gum" and "The Sad Hog"

In this lesson, students will read two short stories and do a story sequencing activity.

You will need: ☐ *Blast Off to Reading!* pages 85-89

☐ *Run, Bug, Run!* book

Review

Review the Phonogram Cards that are behind the Review divider in your student's Reading Review Box. Show the card to your student and have him say the sound(s). If necessary, remind your student of the sound(s).

Review the Word Cards that are behind the Review divider in your student's Reading Review Box. If your student has difficulty reading the word, build the word with letter tiles and have your student sound it out using the procedure shown in Appendix C: Full Blending Procedure.

New Teaching

Story 1: "The Gum"

Read the Warm-Up Sheet for "The Gum"

Remove page 85 from the *Blast Off* activity book.

Have your student practice reading words and phrases that will be encountered in "The Gum."

New Teaching
(continued)

Teach Vocabulary and Activate Prior Knowledge

Point out the illustration of a headstand on the Warm-Up Sheet. "This is a *headstand*. A headstand is when someone actually stands on his head! Have you ever tried to do a headstand?"

"Have you ever made a big mess? How did you clean it up?" Discuss ways to clean up a mess.

"A girl in this next story does a headstand and makes a mess. Let's see how the whole family tries to clean it up."

Read "The Gum"

"Turn to page 109 in your reader and read 'The Gum' aloud." Discuss your student's ideas for the questions below as you come to them.

After page 110: "Look at the illustration. How do you think Peg's gum ends up on the rug?"

After page 115: "The characters have tried many ways to get the gum off the rug, but it won't budge. Do you think they will get it off at the end of the story?"

After reading: "Who do you think has the best idea for getting the gum off the rug? How would *you* do it?"

Complete Activity Sheet

"Let's see if you can remember all the ways the family tried to get the gum off the rug."

Get the Gum!
Remove page 87 from the activity book.

Cut out the story sequencing cards.

Mix up the cards and place them face up on the table. Explain that the cards show the different tools the family in the story uses to get the gum out of the rug. Have your student place the cards in the correct order as they appeared in the story. The student may refer to the story to complete this activity.

Lesson 15: Read "The Gum" and "The Sad Hog"

New Teaching
(continued)

Read the Warm-Up Sheet for "The Sad Hog"

Remove page 89 from the activity book.

Have your student practice reading words and phrases that will be encountered in "The Sad Hog."

Point out the name *Val* in the Names section. "Val is a nickname for Valerie."

Teach Vocabulary and Activate Prior Knowledge

Point out the illustration of a chest on the Warm-Up Sheet. "This is a *chest*. A chest is a big box where you can store things. People often keep chests in the attic or basement to hold old items they want to keep. Other words for chest are *trunk*, *toy chest*, or *toy box*. What kinds of things do you think can be stored in a chest?"

Point out the illustration of a hog on the Warm-Up Sheet. "This is a *hog*. Hog is another name for a pig."

"If your best friend were sad, what would you do to cheer him or her up?" Discuss ways to cheer up a friend.

"In this story, a little girl finds things in an old chest to cheer up her sad pet. Let's see what happens."

New Teaching
(continued)

Read "The Sad Hog"

"Turn to page 119 in your reader and read 'The Sad Hog' aloud." Discuss your student's ideas for the questions below as you come to them.

After page 121: "Why do you think the hog is sad?"

After reading: "Why is the hog happy now?"

Read-Aloud Time

Read a Story or Poem

Read aloud to your student for twenty minutes.

Track Your Progress

Mark the Progress Chart

Have your student mark Lesson 15 on the Progress Chart.

The Gum

Peg got gum on the rug. Ted got a wet rag
Ed got a mop. Ed didn't get the gum.
Dad dig at the gum. Dad didn't get the gum
Mom got a log. Mom hit the gum. Mom
didn't get the gum. Jen got a pig.
The pig got the gum. Yum.

Lesson 15: Read "The Gum" and "The Sad Hog"

Lesson 16 - Letters QU and X

This lesson will teach words containing the phonograms <u>qu</u> and <u>x</u>.

You will need: ☐ Phonogram Cards 25-26   ☐ Word Cards 73-80
☐ Blast Off to Reading! pages 91-94

Before You Begin

Preview the Sounds of the Letters

Your student will learn two new phonograms.

qu The letters <u>q</u> and <u>u</u> work together to make the /kw/ sound as in *queen*. In English words, the letter <u>q</u> is always followed by the letter <u>u</u>, which is why we treat them as one phonogram. In this phonogram, the <u>u</u> doesn't act like a vowel.

x The letter <u>x</u> says /ks/ as in *ax*.

  Listen to the *Phonogram Sounds* app for a demonstration of the phonogram sounds.

Choppy Reading

  It is normal for beginning students to read choppily, one word at a time. They are working very hard at decoding each individual word, so don't expect smooth reading at this stage.

However, you can help your student advance to the next level of fluency in the following two ways.

1. Have your student do a "cold reading" and then a "hot reading" of the sentences on the Practice Sheet. The first time he reads through the sentences, it is a cold reading. Have him read the same sentences several more times to warm up and improve his fluency. When he thinks he is able to read the sentences smoothly, he can announce that

Before You Begin
(continued)

he is ready to do a final "hot reading." Celebrate the difference between the cold reading and the hot reading.

2. Model fluency for your student. Read a sentence aloud with expression, and then have your student read the same sentence after you. This exercise accustoms your student to the feeling of reading at a faster, smoother pace.

At this beginning level, don't be concerned about choppy reading. Just work toward the goal of fluency little by little, and recognize the hard work that your student is accomplishing.

Review

Review the Phonogram Cards that are behind the Review divider in your student's Reading Review Box. Show the card to your student and have him say the sound. If necessary, remind your student of the sound.

Review the Word Cards that are behind the Review divider in your student's Reading Review Box. If your student has difficulty reading the word, build the word with letter tiles and have your student sound it out using the procedure shown in Appendix C: Full Blending Procedure.

New Teaching

Teach New Letter Sounds

Hold up the Phonogram Card for qu.

"See how there are two letters on one card? In English words, the letter q is always followed by the letter u. Together, these letters say /kw/. Repeat after me: /kw/. " *Student repeats.*

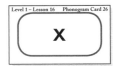

Hold up the Phonogram Card for the letter x.

"The letter x says /ks/. Repeat after me: /ks/." *Student repeats.*

> **Tip!**
> Some students are helped by knowing that the sound of x is made by two sounds spoken in rapid succession: /k/ and /s/.

Mix in several other Phonogram Cards for mixed review and practice until your student can say the sounds accurately. File the new Phonogram Card behind the Review divider in the Reading Review Box.

Lesson 16: Letters QU and X

New Teaching
(continued)

Set out the new letter tiles.

Mix in several other letter tiles for mixed review and practice with the new tiles until your student can say the sounds accurately.

Blend Sounds with Letter Tiles

Build the word *fix* with letter tiles.

"I'll sound out this first word, and then you'll sound out the next word."

Touch the f and say /f/.

Touch the i and say /ĭ/.

Touch the x and say /ks/.

Now go back to the beginning of the word. Slide your finger under the letters f-i-x and say *fix* slowly.

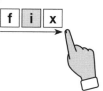

Finally, read the word *fix* at a normal pace, as we do when we speak.

Using the same procedure for blending, have your student sound out the word *quit*.

qu i t

Play "Change the Word"

Keep the word *quit* on the board.

"What is this word?" *Quit.*

"I'm going to change the first letter of this word."

"What does this new word say?" Encourage your student to sound out the new word. *Fit.*

Continue to change one letter at a time to form the following words. Each time, have your student sound out the new word.

fit → fat → fax → tax → wax → ax → as → is → it

> Note that this is the first time you will be changing the vowel during this activity: *fit – fat* and *as – is*. You may wish to point this out to your student.
>
> Also, your student has already learned that the letter s̲ says two sounds. In the words *as* and *is*, s̲ says its second sound, /z/.

Complete Activity Sheet

What's in the Box?

Remove pages 91-92 from the *Blast Off* activity book.

Cut out each of the gift boxes, mix them up, and place them on the table with the words facing up.

To play, have your student select a gift box and turn it over to read the two-word phrase. If your student reads the phrase correctly, he can keep the gift box. If he reads the phrase incorrectly, return the box to the pile for another try.

New Teaching
(continued)

Practice Reading Words

Have your student practice reading the words on Word Cards 73-80.

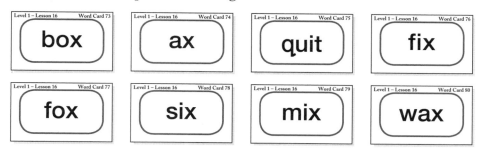

File the Word Cards behind the Review divider of the Reading Review Box.

Practice Fluency

Remove pages 93-94 from the activity book.

Have your student read from the Practice Sheet.

Read-Aloud Time   Read a Story or Poem

Read aloud to your student for twenty minutes.

Track Your Progress

Mark the Progress Chart

Have your student mark Lesson 16 on the Progress Chart.

Hey, there, friend!
Sorry I disappeared for a while,
but I've been on a reconnaissance mission
to the future ... of this book!

And you know what?
You've successfully finished your orbit
of the letters A to Z!

I won't give away all the goodies coming up,
but I will say you are going to be learning
some METEORIC stuff
and reading some
ASTEROID-SMASHING stories!

All systems GO!

Lesson 16: Letters QU and X

Lesson 17 - Read "Pet Ox" and "Fox in a Box"

In this lesson, students will read two short stories and read and create silly sentences.

You will need: ☐ *Blast Off to Reading!* pages 95-98

☐ *Run, Bug, Run!* book

Review

Review the Phonogram Cards that are behind the Review divider in your student's Reading Review Box. Show the card to your student and have him say the sound(s). If necessary, remind your student of the sound(s).

Review the Word Cards that are behind the Review divider in your student's Reading Review Box. If your student has difficulty reading the word, build the word with letter tiles and have your student sound it out using the procedure shown in Appendix C: Full Blending Procedure.

New Teaching

Story 1: "Pet Ox"

Complete Activity Sheet

"Imagine if you kept a snake in your refrigerator or an elephant under your couch! In this activity, you'll make silly sentences about animals in strange places."

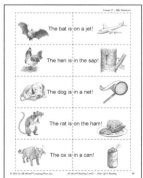

Silly Sentences

Remove pages 95-96 from the *Blast Off* activity book.

Cut out the animal and place cards. Note that animal cards are marked with a paw print on the back and place cards are marked with a compass rose.

Shuffle and place the cards face down in two piles, one for animals and one for places. Have your student draw one card from the animal pile and

New Teaching
(continued)

one card from the place pile and read the resulting silly sentence.

Continue until your student has read all the silly sentences.

Read the Warm-Up Sheet for "Pet Ox"

Don't Forget

You will need the flip side of this Warm-Up Sheet for the next story, "Fox in a Box." If you won't be completing that portion of the lesson today, return this Warm-Up Sheet to the activity book for safekeeping.

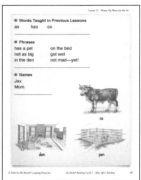

Remove page 97 from the activity book.

Have your student practice reading words and phrases that will be encountered in "Pet Ox."

Point out the name *Jax* in the Names section. "Jax is a nickname for Jackson."

Today's Warm-Up Sheet includes a dash (—). Explain that a dash is a line that indicates a pause in speech or an unfinished sentence. Dashes can be used in the middle or at the end of a sentence.

Teach Vocabulary and Activate Prior Knowledge

Point out the illustration of a pen on the Warm-Up Sheet. "A *pen* is a kind of enclosure for animals. Farmers use pens to keep their pigs, for example."

Point out the illustration of an ox on the Warm-Up Sheet. "An *ox* is a large animal like a cow or bull. An ox is very strong and is often used to pull or carry heavy loads. Where do you think a farmer would keep his ox?"

"If you could have any animal in the world as a pet, no matter how big or small, what would it be? Why?"

"Would you let that pet in the house or keep it outside? Why?"

"In this next story, a boy lets an unusual pet inside the house. Let's see what happens."

New Teaching
(continued)

Read "Pet Ox"

"Turn to page 129 in your reader and read 'Pet Ox' aloud." Discuss your student's ideas for the questions below as you come to them.

After page 133: "Do you think Jax is supposed to have the ox in the house? Why or why not?"

After page 135: "Why is Mom mad?"

After reading: "Go back and look at the illustrations on pages 131-134. What do Jax and the ox do on each page that might make Mom mad?"

Story 2: "Fox in a Box"

Read the Warm-Up Sheet for "Fox in a Box"

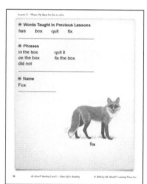

Remove page 98 from the activity book.

Have your student practice reading words and phrases that will be encountered in "Fox in a Box."

Activate Prior Knowledge

"Have you ever played with an empty box? What kinds of things can you do with a big box?" Discuss creative ways to play with a box.

"In the story you are about to read, a fox has lots of fun with a box."

New Teaching
(continued)

Read "Fox in a Box"

"Turn to page 139 in your reader and read 'Fox in a Box' aloud." Discuss your student's ideas for the questions below as you come to them.

After page 141: "Where do you think this box comes from? How does it end up in the woods?"

After page 146: "Why does Fox spit out the piece of box?"

Read-Aloud Time

Read a Story or Poem

Read aloud to your student for twenty minutes.

Track Your Progress

Mark the Progress Chart

Have your student mark Lesson 17 on the Progress Chart.

Lesson 18 - Consonant Team TH

This lesson will teach the concept of consonant teams and words containing both sounds of consonant team th.

You will need:
- [ ] Phonogram Card 27
- [ ] Letter tile th
- [ ] Consonant Teams label
- [ ] Blast Off to Reading! pages 99-104
- [ ] Word Cards 81-88
- [ ] spatula

Before You Begin

Preview Consonant Teams

When two consonants work together to make one sound, we call them a consonant team. Another common term for this is *consonant digraph*.

Six consonant teams will be taught in Level 1: th as in *three* and *then*; sh as in *ship*; ch as in *child*, *school*, and *chef*; ck as in *duck*; ng as in *king*; and nk as in *thank*.

Preview Consonant Team TH

th Today you will be teaching the consonant team th.

Depending on the word, th says /th/ as in *three* or /th̶/ as in *then*. You will notice that there is a strikethrough on the th in the second sound: /th̶/. This strikethrough is used to differentiate between the two sounds of th. The /th/ is considered an *unvoiced* sound, while the /th̶/ is considered a *voiced* sound because we use our vocal cords to say it.

Your student will learn both sounds of th in this lesson. Examples incude:

| /th/: | bath | moth | thin |
| /th̶/: | than | this | them |

 Listen to the *Phonogram Sounds* app for a demonstration of the phonogram sounds.

Place the Consonant Teams Label on the Board

We will use the Consonant Teams label to organize consonant teams. Place the label below the alphabet row, and place the <u>th</u> tile below the label.

To see what the magnetic white board will look like after all of the Level 1 consonant teams have been placed on the board, refer to Appendix L.

Avoid Making Corrections Too Soon

When your student misreads a word in a sentence, resist the temptation to correct him immediately. Let him reach the end of the sentence before you interrupt, giving him the chance to realize on his own that he made a mistake.

For example, if your student reads *The hot sat with a thud,* he will probably self-correct because the sentence obviously doesn't make sense. He will look back to see where his error is and reread the sentence correctly as *The hog sat with a thud.* If he does continue reading without correcting himself, ask him if the sentence he just read makes sense.

When you interrupt your student immediately after he makes an error, he is deprived of the opportunity to monitor what he is reading for meaning. In the example above, the phrase *The hot...* does make sense in itself, as it could be *The hot day* or *The hot lunch.* If you give your student time to reach the end of the sentence, though, it will most likely be clear to him that he has misread a word.

Review

Review the Phonogram Cards that are behind the Review divider in your student's Reading Review Box. Show the card to your student and have him say the sound. If necessary, remind your student of the sound.

Review the Word Cards that are behind the Review divider in your student's Reading Review Box. If your student has difficulty reading the word, build the word with letter tiles and have your student sound it out using the procedure shown in Appendix C: Full Blending Procedure.

New Teaching

Teach New Letter Sounds

Hold up the Phonogram Card for the consonant team th.

"See how there are two letters on one card? The two letters work together to make one sound."

"These letters can say /th/, or they can say /t̶h̶/."

"Repeat after me: /th/–/t̶h̶/." *Student repeats.*

Mix in several other Phonogram Cards for mixed review and practice until your student can say the sounds accurately. File the new Phonogram Card behind the Review divider in the Reading Review Box.

Set out the new letter tile. `th`

Mix in several other letter tiles for mixed review and practice with the new tile until your student can say the sounds accurately.

Blend Sounds with Letter Tiles

"When we read words with th, we try the first sound first. If that doesn't make a word you recognize, then try the second sound of th."

Build the word *them* with letter tiles. `th` `e` `m`

"I'll sound out this first word, and then you'll sound out the next word."

"First I try the first sound of <u>th</u>." Touch the <u>th</u> and say /th/.

"Then I sound out the rest of the word."

Touch the <u>e</u> and say /ĕ/, then touch the <u>m</u> and say /m/.

Now go back to the beginning of the word and blend the sounds together, using the first sound of <u>th</u>. Slide your finger under the letters <u>th</u>-<u>e</u>-<u>m</u> and say /thĕm/.

"With the first sound of <u>th</u>, this word doesn't sound like a word I recognize. So now I try the second sound of <u>th</u>, /th/."

Repeat the steps above, using the second sound of <u>th</u>. Then go back and blend the sounds together. Slide your finger under the letters <u>th</u>-<u>e</u>-<u>m</u> and say *them*.

"So this word says *them*. It uses /th/, the second sound of <u>th</u>."

"Now it's your turn. Remember to always try the first sound of <u>th</u> first."

Using the same procedure for blending, have your student sound out the words *this* and *bath*. Be sure your student tries the first sound of <u>th</u> first, then the second sound.

Play "Change the Word"

Keep the word *bath* on the board. | b | a | th |

"I'm going to change the first letter of this word."

Lesson 18: Consonant Team TH

New Teaching
(continued)

"What does this new word say?" Encourage your student to sound out the new word. *Math.*

Continue to change one letter at a time to form the following words. Each time, have your student sound out the new word.

math → path → pat → pan → an → in → thin

This next sequence contains the second sound of <u>th</u>. Change one letter at a time to form the following words.

that → than → then → them

Complete Activity Sheet

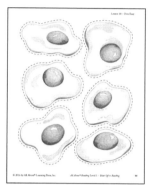

Over Easy
Remove pages 99-102 from the *Blast Off* activity book.

Cut out the eggs. Color the yolks yellow, if desired.

Place several eggs sunny side up in a pan. Have your student use a spatula to flip over the eggs, one at a time, and read the word.

If your student reads the word correctly, he can keep the fried egg. If he reads the word incorrectly, he should put the egg back in the pan and try again.

Practice Reading Words

Have your student practice reading the words on Word Cards 81-88.

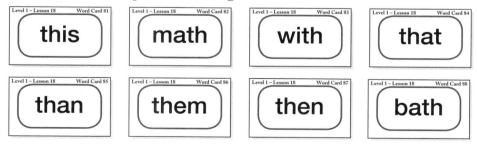

File the Word Cards behind the Review divider of the Reading Review Box.

New Teaching
(continued)

Practice Fluency

Remove pages 103-104 from the activity book.

Have your student read from the Practice Sheet.

Read-Aloud Time

Read a Story or Poem

Read aloud to your student for twenty minutes.

Track Your Progress

Mark the Progress Chart

Have your student mark Lesson 18 on the Progress Chart.

Lesson 18: Consonant Team TH

Lesson 19 - Read "Get Them!" and "The Red Pen"

In this lesson, students will read two short stories and complete a character motivation activity.

You will need: ☐ *Blast Off to Reading!* pages 105-108

☐ *Run, Bug, Run!* book

Review

Review the Phonogram Cards that are behind the Review divider in your student's Reading Review Box. Show the card to your student and have him say the sound(s). If necessary, remind your student of the sound(s).

Review the Word Cards that are behind the Review divider in your student's Reading Review Box. If your student has difficulty reading the word, build the word with letter tiles and have your student sound it out using the procedure shown in Appendix C: Full Blending Procedure.

If you are using *Reading Games with Ziggy the Zebra*, you can play "Caving with Ziggy" for a fun way to review the Phonogram Cards and Word Cards.

New Teaching

Story 1: "Get Them!"

Complete Activity Sheet

"You probably have a reason for doing everything you do. This is called your *motivation*. In this activity, you'll discover the reasons various animals do what they do."

Why Did They Do That?
Remove page 105 from the *Blast Off* activity book.

Cut out the cards and place them face down on the table. Have your student draw one card at a time and then answer one of the character motivation questions below.

New Teaching
(continued)

Q: Why is the cat licking her paw?
Possible answers: She wants to be clean; it hurts.

Q: Why does the monkey want the banana?
Possible answer: He's hungry.

Q: Why is the seal balancing the ball?
Possible answers: He's been trained; to make people laugh.

Q: Why does the bird have a twig in her mouth?
Possible answer: She wants to build a nest.

Q: Why is the meerkat standing guard?
Possible answers: He wants to protect his family; to make sure enemies stay away.

Q: Why is the lion roaring?
Possible answers: He wants to show who is boss; he wants to scare others away.

Discuss your student's answers.

Read the Warm-Up Sheet for "Get Them!"

Don't Forget You will need the flip side of this Warm-Up Sheet for the next story, "The Red Pen." If you won't be completing that portion of the lesson today, return this Warm-Up Sheet to the activity book for safekeeping.

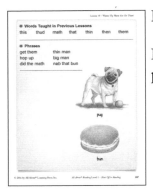

Remove page 107 from the activity book.

Have your student practice reading words and phrases that will be encountered in "Get Them!"

Teach Vocabulary and Activate Prior Knowledge

Point out the illustration of a pug on the Warm-Up Sheet. "A *pug* is a small dog with a flat nose and a very wrinkled face. There is a pug in today's story."

Point out the illustration of a bun on the Warm-Up Sheet. "A *bun* is a small cake or bread. Have you ever had a cinnamon bun or a dinner bun with butter? The pug in the next story is very fond of buns!"

Lesson 19: Read "Get Them!" and "The Red Pen"

New Teaching
(continued)

"Have you ever been on a team or in a group to play a game or do a project? How did it go?" Discuss any experience your student has had as part of a team.

"Do you prefer to do things by yourself or with a team or group? Why?"

"In this next story, a pug gets help from a group of people. Let's see what happens."

Read "Get Them!"

"Turn to page 151 in your reader and read 'Get Them!' aloud." Discuss your student's ideas for the questions below as you come to them.

After page 154: "Hopping doesn't work. What else could the pug do to get the bun?"

After page 158: "What is the pug going to do with all these people?"

> You may need to explain the word *nab* on page 159 to your student. *Nab* means *to grab* or *to catch.*

After page 161: "Do you think the pug is going to get away with the bun? Why or why not?"

Story 2: "The Red Pen"

Read the Warm-Up Sheet for "The Red Pen"

Remove page 108 from in the activity book.

Have your student practice reading words and phrases that will be encountered in "The Red Pen."

Point out the name *Tex* in the Names section. "Tex is a nickname for Texas."

New Teaching (continued)	**Teach Vocabulary and Activate Prior Knowledge**

Point out the illustration of a jet on the Warm-Up Sheet. "A *jet* is a large, very fast airplane."

Point out the illustration of a bog on the Warm-Up Sheet. "A *bog* is an area where the ground is wet, muddy, and spongy. It is hard to walk in a bog!"

"If you could be anything for a day, like a bird or a tree or a cloud, what would you be?" Discuss what your student would do during his day as his chosen object.

"The boy in the story you are about to read has a big imagination. Let's see what he would like to be."

Read "The Red Pen"

"Turn to page 165 in your reader and read 'The Red Pen' aloud." Discuss your student's ideas for the questions below as you come to them.

After reading: "Tex imagines that he is many things. Why do you think he would like to be a pen? A log? A box?"

"Look at the illustrations on pages 167 and 176. Based on the items in Tex's bedroom, what are some things that Tex likes to do?" *Possible answers: Play basketball, play guitar, listen to music, draw, read, play with his dog.*

Read-Aloud Time	**Read a Story or Poem**

Read aloud to your student for twenty minutes.

Track Your Progress	**Mark the Progress Chart**

Have your student mark Lesson 19 on the Progress Chart.

Lesson 19: Read "Get Them!" and "The Red Pen"

Lesson 20 - Consonant Team SH

This lesson will teach words containing the consonant team sh.

You will need: ☐ Phonogram Card 28   ☐ Blast Off to Reading! pages 109-116
☐ Letter tile sh   ☐ Word Cards 89-96

Before You Begin

Preview Consonant Team SH

sh   The consonant team sh says /sh/ as in *ship*.

You may wish to help your student remember the sound of /sh/ by showing him how to hold his finger to his lips and say "shhh."

 Listen to the *Phonogram Sounds* app for a demonstration of the phonogram sound.

Store the new tile under the following label:

Consonant Teams

sh

Avoid Excessive Feedback

In Lesson 18, we talked about why it is important to let your student finish a sentence even after he has misread a word. This practice encourages your student to monitor for meaning, asking himself "Does this sentence make sense?"

On the flip side of the coin is the teacher who offers immediate feedback, constantly interrupting the student for every misread word. Too often, such a stream of feedback causes the student to become dependent on the teacher to confirm that the word or phrase he just read is correct. The reader waits for the teacher to nod or say "good" or "uh-huh," which then becomes a cycle: the student reads a word or two, waits for affirmation, then reads a few more words. This stop-and-go cycle works against the development of fluency.

Before You Begin
(continued)

If you feel yourself falling into this negative routine with your student, let him know that from now on, you will give feedback after the sentence has been completed, instead of during his reading.

Review

Review the Phonogram Cards that are behind the Review divider in your student's Reading Review Box. Show the card to your student and have him say the sound. If necessary, remind your student of the sound.

Review the Word Cards that are behind the Review divider in your student's Reading Review Box. If your student has difficulty reading the word, build the word with letter tiles and have your student sound it out using the procedure shown in Appendix C: Full Blending Procedure.

New Teaching

Teach New Letter Sounds

Teach the Phonogram Card for the consonant team <u>sh</u>.

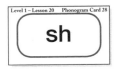

1. Hold up the Phonogram Card and demonstrate the sound.
2. Have your student repeat the sound.

Mix in several other Phonogram Cards for mixed review and practice until your student can say the sounds accurately. File the new Phonogram Card behind the Review divider in the Reading Review Box.

Set out the new letter tile. **sh**

Mix in several other letter tiles for mixed review and practice with the new tile until your student can say the sound accurately.

New Teaching
(continued)

Blend Sounds with Letter Tiles

Build the word *shut* with letter tiles.

"I'll sound out this first word, and then you'll sound out the next word."

Touch the s̲h̲ and say /*sh*/.

Touch the u̲ and say /ŭ/.

Touch the t̲ and say /*t*/.

Now go back to the beginning of the word. Slide your finger under the letters s̲h̲-u̲-t̲ and say *shut* slowly.

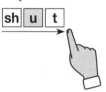

Finally, read the word *shut* at a normal pace, as we do when we speak.

Using the same procedure for blending, have your student sound out the word *cash*.

c a sh

Discuss the Exclamation "Sh!"

"Has anyone ever said *Sh!* to you? What does it mean?" *Be quiet.*

Write the word "Sh!" on a piece of paper and show it to your student. "*Sh!* is spelled just like it sounds: s̲-h̲. It is usually followed by an exclamation point."

"Sh!" is used in future stories, so preteaching it now will give your student a head start when he encounters the word in his reading.

Play "Change the Word"

Build the word *wish*.

"What is this word?" *Wish.*

"I'm going to change the first letter of this word."

"What does this new word say?" Encourage your student to sound out the new word. *Fish.*

Continue to change one letter at a time to form the following words. Each time, have your student sound out the new word.

fish → dish → dip → ship → shop

Complete Activity Sheet

Word Flippers for SH

Remove pages 109-113 from the *Blast Off* activity book.

Refer to Appendix E for assembly instructions.

Have your student flip through the book randomly, reading the words that are formed.

Practice Reading Words

Have your student practice reading the words on Word Cards 89-96.

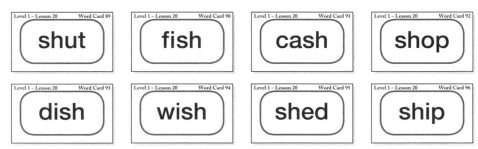

File the Word Cards behind the Review divider of the Reading Review Box.

New Teaching
(continued)

Practice Fluency

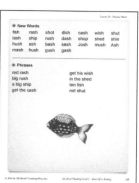

Remove pages 115-116 from the activity book.

Have your student read from the Practice Sheet.

Read-Aloud Time

Read a Story or Poem

Read aloud to your student for twenty minutes.

Track Your Progress

Mark the Progress Chart

Have your student mark Lesson 20 on the Progress Chart.

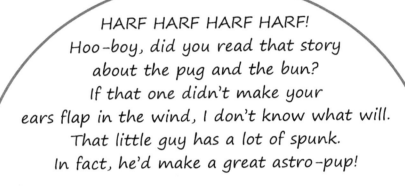

HARF HARF HARF HARF!
Hoo-boy, did you read that story
about the pug and the bun?
If that one didn't make your
ears flap in the wind, I don't know what will.
That little guy has a lot of spunk.
In fact, he'd make a great astro-pup!

Oh, but SH!
I forgot this SH phonogram makes us whisper ...
so I'm going to tiptoe back to my spaceSHip,
SHut the door, and have
a nice diSH of space kibbles.

I wiSH you could join me!

142

Lesson 20: Consonant Team SH

Lesson 21 - Read "Run!" and "Six Fish"

In this lesson, students will read two short stories and learn about story settings.

You will need: ☐ *Blast Off to Reading!* pages 117-122

☐ *Run, Bug, Run!* book   ☐ Optional: map or globe

Review

Review the Phonogram Cards that are behind the Review divider in your student's Reading Review Box. Show the card to your student and have him say the sound(s). If necessary, remind your student of the sound(s).

Review the Word Cards that are behind the Review divider in your student's Reading Review Box. If your student has difficulty reading the word, build the word with letter tiles and have your student sound it out using the procedure shown in Appendix C: Full Blending Procedure.

New Teaching

Story 1: "Run!"

Complete Activity Sheet

"You know that the place where a story happens is called the setting. In this activity, you'll put various objects in their correct setting."

In the Right Place
Remove pages 117-119 from the *Blast Off* activity book.

Cut out the cards on page 119.

Mix up the cards and place them face down on the table. Have your student draw one card at a time and then decide which setting that card belongs in, either the indoor setting or the outdoor setting.

Continue until all the cards have been placed in the appropriate setting.

New Teaching
(continued)

Don't Forget

You will need the flip side of this Warm-Up Sheet for the next story, "Six Fish." If you won't be completing that portion of the lesson today, return this Warm-Up Sheet to the activity book for safekeeping.

Read the Warm-Up Sheet for "Run!"

Remove page 121 from the activity book.

Have your student practice reading words and phrases that will be encountered in "Run!"

Teach Vocabulary and Activate Prior Knowledge

Point out the illustration of a cub on the Warm-Up Sheet. "A *cub* is a young bear. The word is also used for other baby animals like tigers, but in today's story, it refers to a baby bear."

Point out the illustration of a llama on the Warm-Up Sheet. "This is a *llama*. A llama is a domesticated animal in the camel family. Llamas are often raised for their soft, woolly fleece."

"Have you ever been scared by a shadow or an object that turned out to not be scary? Tell me about it."

"If you were in the woods and thought you saw a bear cub or other large animal, what would you do?"

"The boy in this story thinks he sees something in the field. Let's see what happens."

Read "Run!"

"Turn to page 179 in your reader and read 'Run!' aloud." Discuss your student's ideas for the questions below as you come to them.

After page 180: "Do you think they really see a cub outside? What else could it be?"

After reading: "Look at the illustrations on pages 183, 184, and 188. Do you think the setting of this story is in the United States or a different country?"

Lesson 21: Read "Run!" and "Six Fish"

New Teaching
(continued)

Find Bolivia on a map or globe. "This story is set in Bolivia, a country in South America. Bolivians harvest quinoa in fields like this, bent over the crops. Quinoa is a type of grain used for food or to make flour."

Story 2: "Six Fish"

Read the Warm-Up Sheet for "Six Fish"

Remove page 122 from the activity book.

Have your student practice reading words and phrases that will be encountered in "Six Fish."

Point out the name *Ash* in the Names section. "Ash is a nickname for Ashton."

Teach Vocabulary and Activate Prior Knowledge

Point out the illustration of cash on the Warm-Up Sheet. "*Cash* is another word for money. It includes both coins and paper money."

"Have you ever received cash for a job you did? What was the job?"

"Did you save the cash or did you buy something with it?"

"What kind of animal do you think makes the best pet?" Discuss your student's chosen animal and why it makes a good pet.

"Let's see what kind of pet the girl in this story chooses."

New Teaching
(continued)

Read "Six Fish"

"Turn to page 191 in your reader and read 'Six Fish' aloud." Discuss your student's ideas for the questions below as you come to them.

After page 199: "Which pet do you think Beth will choose? Why?"

After reading: "Beth does three jobs to get cash. Look at the illustrations on pages 192-195. What are the jobs? What goes wrong with each one?"

"Look at the illustration on page 199. Based on the drawings and the names of the fish, what kind of personality do you think each fish has?"

Read-Aloud Time

Read a Story or Poem

Read aloud to your student for twenty minutes.

Track Your Progress

Mark the Progress Chart

Have your student mark Lesson 21 on the Progress Chart.

Lesson 22 - Consonant Team CH

This lesson will **teach** words containing the consonant team _ch_.

You will need: ☐ Phonogram Card 29   ☐ _Blast Off to Reading!_ pages 123-131

☐ Letter tile _ch_   ☐ Word Cards 97-102

Before You Begin

Preview Consonant Team CH

| ch | The consonant team _ch_ has three sounds: /ch/–/k/–/sh/. In this lesson, your student will learn the first and most common sound, /ch/ as in _child_. The other two sounds will be taught in Lesson 48.

Listen to the _Phonogram Sounds_ app for a demonstration of the phonogram sounds.

Store the new tile under the following label:

| Consonant Teams |

| ch |

Review

Review the Phonogram Cards that are behind the Review divider in your student's Reading Review Box. Show the card to your student and have him say the sound. If necessary, remind your student of the sound.

Review the Word Cards that are behind the Review divider in your student's Reading Review Box. If your student has difficulty reading the word, build the word with letter tiles and have your student sound it out using the procedure shown in Appendix C: Full Blending Procedure.

New Teaching

Teach New Letter Sounds

Teach the Phonogram Card for the consonant team <u>ch</u>.

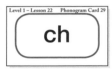

1. Hold up the Phonogram Card and demonstrate the first sound, /ch/.
2. Have your student repeat the sound.

Mix in several other Phonogram Cards for mixed review and practice until your student can say the sounds accurately. File the new Phonogram Card behind the Review divider in the Reading Review Box.

Set out the new letter tile.   ch

Mix in several other letter tiles for mixed review and practice with the new tile until your student can say the sound accurately.

Blend Sounds with Letter Tiles

Build the word *chop* with letter tiles.

"I'll sound out this first word, and then you'll sound out the next word."

Touch the <u>ch</u> and say */ch/*.

Touch the <u>o</u> and say */ŏ/*.

Touch the <u>p</u> and say */p/*.

New Teaching
(continued)

Now go back to the beginning of the word. Slide your finger under the letters <u>ch</u>-<u>o</u>-p and say *chop* slowly.

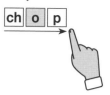

Finally, read the word *chop* at a normal pace, as we do when we speak.

Using the same procedure for blending, have your student sound out the word *rich*.

Play "Change the Word"

Build the word *chin*. ch i n

"What is this word?" *Chin.*

"I'm going to change the last letter of this word."

"What does this new word say?" Encourage your student to sound out the new word. *Chip.*

Continue to change one letter at a time to form the following words. Each time, have your student sound out the new word.

chip → chop → chap → chat

New Teaching
(continued)

Complete Activity Sheets

The "Little Mouse" activity sheet provides practice with words containing <u>ch</u>.

Little Mouse

Remove pages 123-125 from the *Blast Off* activity book.

Color the cheese and mouse, if desired. Cut out the mouse and the cheese cards as indicated.

Set out the twelve pieces of cheese with the words facing down.

You and your student take turns being the mouse. The mouse sneaks up to the pile of cheese and takes one piece.

The mouse reads the word on the piece of cheese that was selected. If the word is read correctly, the mouse keeps the cheese. If the word is read incorrectly, it goes back into the cheese pile.

The "Mail a Letter" activity sheet provides mixed review of words containing <u>th</u>, <u>sh</u>, and <u>ch</u>. You may choose to do this second activity sheet during a different lesson if your student is tiring.

Mail a Letter

Remove pages 127-128 from the activity book.

Make a small slot in each mailbox by cutting along the dotted line on the back.

Cut out the "letters" on the bottom of the page and place them in a pile with the words facing down.

Have your student draw one letter at a time, turn it over, read the word, and decide which mailbox he needs to deliver it to. He may then slip the letter into the correct mailbox.

Continue until your student has delivered all the letters.

New Teaching
(continued)

Practice Reading Words

Have your student practice reading the words on Word Cards 97-102.

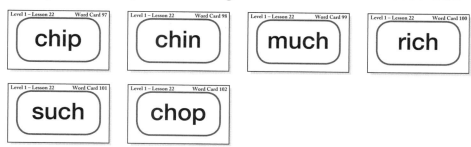

File the Word Cards behind the Review divider of the Reading Review Box.

Practice Fluency

Remove pages 129-131 from the activity book.

Have your student read from the Practice Sheet.

Read-Aloud Time   ## Read a Story or Poem

Read aloud to your student for twenty minutes.

Track Your Progress

Mark the Progress Chart

Have your student mark Lesson 22 on the Progress Chart.

A-rooooooooo!
I can hardly hear youuuuuuuuuuuu!
Every astro-dog in orbit is reviewing flashcards,
and they are really woofing it up!
I can barely hear myself howl.

Have you been reviewing yours?

(See you soooooooon!)

Lesson 23 - Read "The Tub" and "Get the Moth, Meg!"

In this lesson, students will read two short stories and use illustrations to retell a story.

You will need: ☐ *Blast Off to Reading!* pages 133-137

☐ *Run, Bug, Run!* book ☐ Optional: map or globe

Review

Review the Phonogram Cards that are behind the Review divider in your student's Reading Review Box. Show the card to your student and have him say the sound(s). If necessary, remind your student of the sound(s).

Review the Word Cards that are behind the Review divider in your student's Reading Review Box. If your student has difficulty reading the word, build the word with letter tiles and have your student sound it out using the procedure shown in Appendix C: Full Blending Procedure.

New Teaching

Story 1: "The Tub"

Read the Warm-Up Sheet for "The Tub"

Remove page 133 from the *Blast Off* activity book.

Have your student practice reading words and phrases that will be encountered in "The Tub."

Teach Vocabulary and Activate Prior Knowledge

Point out the illustration of a zig-zag on the Warm-Up Sheet. "This is a *zig-zag*. A zig-zag is a line that has a lot of sharp turns."

New Teaching
(continued)

Point out the illustration of a spider monkey on the Warm-Up Sheet. "This is a *spider monkey*. Spider monkeys are small monkeys that live in the rain forests of Costa Rica."

Find Costa Rica on a map or globe. "This story is set in Costa Rica, a country in Central America. The story features a couple of spider monkeys having a great time with their water toys."

"What are your favorite toys to play with in the bathtub or at the beach?"

"Let's see what these monkeys do for fun."

Read "The Tub"

"Turn to page 203 in your reader and read 'The Tub' aloud." Discuss your student's ideas for the question below when you come to it.

After page 207: "What do you think they'll put in the tub next? What would you put in it?"

Complete Activity Sheet

"Now it's your turn to tell the story of the tub."

Tell Me a Story
Remove page 135 from the activity book.

Cut out the cards on the top of the page.

Have your student retell the story "The Tub," using the illustrated cards as props. As each item appears in your student's story, he may add it to the illustration of the tub.

Continue until your student has finished his story.

New Teaching
(continued)

Read the Warm-Up Sheet for "Get the Moth, Meg!"

Remove page 137 from the activity book.

Have your student practice reading words and phrases that will be encountered in "Get the Moth, Meg!"

Note that the exclamation "Sh!" is reviewed on this Warm-Up Sheet.

The exclamation is used in the story "Get the Moth, Meg!"

Teach Vocabulary and Activate Prior Knowledge

Point out the illustration of a water tap on the Warm-Up Sheet. "This is a *water tap. Tap* is another word for *faucet.*"

Point out the illustration of a moth on the Warm-Up Sheet. "A *moth* is an insect with two pairs of wings. Unlike butterflies, moths don't have antennae, and their colors are not as bright. Moths are mostly nocturnal. Do you ever see moths fluttering around your porch light at night?"

"Did you ever have a mosquito or fly that just wouldn't leave you alone? Maybe it kept buzzing around your head! What could you have done to try to catch it?" Discuss your student's experience and how he could have caught the insect.

"Let's see what happens when the girl in this story tries to catch a moth."

New Teaching	Read "Get the Moth, Meg!"

New Teaching
(continued)

Read "Get the Moth, Meg!"

"Turn to page 211 in your reader and read 'Get the Moth, Meg!' aloud."
Discuss your student's ideas for the questions below as you come to them.

After page 214: "Is the moth really doing something bad? Why does Meg think it is bad?"

After page 218: "Why is Meg mad?"

Read-Aloud Time

Read a Story or Poem

Read aloud to your student for twenty minutes.

Track Your Progress

Mark the Progress Chart

Have your student mark Lesson 23 on the Progress Chart.

Lesson 24 - Words with Final Blends

This lesson will teach words containing consonant blends at the end, as well as the Leap Word <u>was</u>.

You will need: ☐ *Blast Off to Reading!* pages 139-152

☐ Word Cards 103-112

Before You Begin

A consonant blend is different from a consonant team. In a consonant blend, each letter retains its own sound. In consonant teams, such as <u>th</u>, <u>sh</u>, and <u>ch</u>, two letters combine to make a completely new sound.

Preview Consonant Blends

In this lesson, your student will learn to read words with consonant blends.

A consonant blend consists of two sounds that are said together quickly. For example, the word *lamp* has a consonant blend at the end. The /m/ and /p/ sounds are said in rapid succession, but each consonant keeps its own sound.

A blend at the end of a word is called a **final blend**. Final blends are easier to read than blends at the beginning of the word, so we will introduce final blends first. Read the following examples and listen for the blends.

dust   help   risk   felt   bump

Words with consonant blends will be decoded using the same blending procedure that your student is already using. Touch each letter and say its sound, slowly at first, and then fast like you would in everyday speech.

Some phonics programs teach blends as a unit. For example, the blends <u>sp</u> and <u>nd</u> would be taught as their own sounds on letter tiles or flashcards. But that method requires much more memory work on the part of the student because the student would have to memorize dozens of blends. It is much simpler to have the student learn the basic phonograms and blend them to sound out words.

Reminder about the Practice Sheets

The goal of the Practice Sheets is to help your student achieve *automaticity*. Automaticity—or automatic word recognition—means that words are recognized at a glance. Automaticity enables your student to read more fluently. When he doesn't have to laboriously decode each and every word, he can read smoothly and with greater comprehension.

Because there are so many possible final blends, this lesson contains several additional Practice Sheets. Please remember that the Practice Sheets aren't meant to be completed in a single sitting! It is critical to stop before your student fatigues. You may take several days or weeks to cover all of the activities in this lesson, depending on your circumstances. See Appendix F for ideas on using the Practice Sheets.

Review

Review the Phonogram Cards that are behind the Review divider in your student's Reading Review Box. Show the card to your student and have him say the sound. If necessary, remind your student of the sound.

Review the Word Cards that are behind the Review divider in your student's Reading Review Box. If your student has difficulty reading the word, build the word with letter tiles and have your student sound it out using the procedure shown in Appendix C: Full Blending Procedure.

New Teaching

Blend Sounds with Letter Tiles

Build the word *land* with letter tiles. | l | a | n | d |

"Sometimes there are two consonants at the end of a word, as in the word *land*. Listen and watch as I blend the letters in this word: l-a-n-d."

Touch the l and say /l/.

Touch the a and say /ă/.

Touch the n and say /n/.

New Teaching
(continued)

Touch the <u>d</u> and say /d/.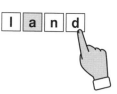

Now go back to the beginning of the word. Slide your finger under the letters <u>l</u>-<u>a</u>-<u>n</u>-<u>d</u> and say *land* slowly.

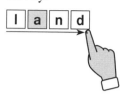

Finally, read the word *land* at a normal pace, as we do when we speak.

Using the same procedure for blending, have your student sound out the word *best*.

| b | e | s | t |

Decode Words Containing Two-Letter Phonograms

Build the word *lunch* with letter tiles. | l | u | n | ch |

"Sometimes one of the sounds at the end of a word is a consonant team, as in the word *lunch*. Listen and watch as I blend the letters in this word: <u>l</u>-<u>u</u>-<u>n</u>-<u>ch</u>."

Touch the <u>l</u> and say /l/.

Touch the <u>u</u> and say /ŭ/.

Touch the <u>n</u> and say /n/.

New Teaching
(continued)

Touch the <u>ch</u> and say /ch/.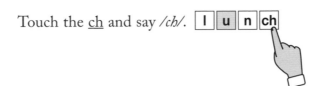

Now go back to the beginning of the word. Slide your finger under the letters <u>l</u>-<u>u</u>-<u>n</u>-<u>ch</u> and say *lunch* slowly.

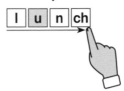

Finally, read the word *lunch* at a normal pace, as we do when we speak.

Using the same procedure for blending, have your student sound out the word *tenth*.

| t | e | n | th |

Complete Activity Sheets

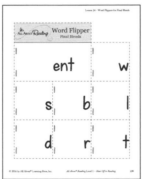

<u>Word Flippers for Final Blends</u>
Remove pages 139-145 from the *Blast Off* activity book.

Refer to Appendix E for assembly instructions.

Have your student turn the pages and read the words that are formed.

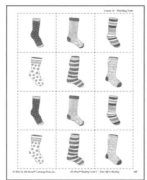

<u>Matching Socks</u>
Remove pages 147-148 from the activity book.

Cut out the individual socks and put them in random order on the table, with the words facing down.

Have your student find two socks that match, and then read the words on the back of the socks.

New Teaching
(continued)

Practice Reading Words

Have your student practice reading the words on Word Cards 103-111.

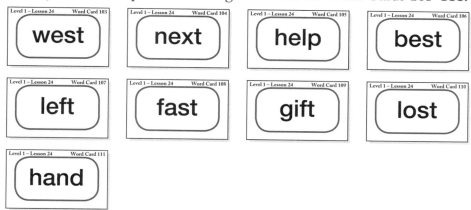

File the Word Cards behind the Review divider of the Reading Review Box.

Teach a Leap Word: *was*

Show Word Card 112 to your student.

"Most words follow the rules and say the sounds that we expect them to say. But there are a few words that do not. Here is one of those words."

"This word is *was*, as in *She was a lion tamer*."

Point to the <u>a</u>. "The <u>a</u> doesn't say the sound we expect it to."

Review this Leap Word several times today and then file it behind the Review divider in the Reading Review Box.

New Teaching
(continued)

Practice Fluency

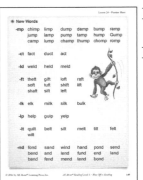

Remove pages 149-152 from the activity book.

Have your student read from the Practice Sheet.

Read-Aloud Time

Read a Story or Poem

Read aloud to your student for twenty minutes.

Track Your Progress

Mark the Progress Chart

Have your student mark Lesson 24 on the Progress Chart.

Lesson 24: Words with Final Blends

Lesson 25 - Read "Tin Raft" and "Lost in the Bog"

In this lesson, students will read two short stories and practice matching text and illustrations.

You will need: ☐ *Blast Off to Reading!* pages 153-159

☐ *The Runt Pig* book

Before You Begin

Today your student will read the first story in the second reader, *The Runt Pig*.

The stories in *The Runt Pig* have been specially written to increase your student's fluency and comprehension skills even further. The wide variety will help keep your student interested and motivated.

Remember to check out the tips in Appendix J if your student runs into difficulties while reading the stories.

Review

Review the Phonogram Cards that are behind the Review divider in your student's Reading Review Box. Show the card to your student and have him say the sound(s). If necessary, remind your student of the sound(s).

Review the Word Cards that are behind the Review divider in your student's Reading Review Box. If your student has difficulty reading the word, build the word with letter tiles and have your student sound it out using the procedure shown in Appendix C: Full Blending Procedure.

New Teaching

Read the Warm-Up Sheet for "Tin Raft"

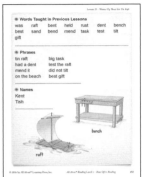

Remove page 153 from the *Blast Off* activity book.

Have your student practice reading words and phrases that will be encountered in "Tin Raft."

Point out the name *Tish* in the Names section. "Tish is a nickname for Patricia."

Teach Vocabulary and Activate Prior Knowledge

Point out the illustration of a raft on the Warm-Up Sheet. "A *raft* is a flat structure that floats and is used as a boat. Rafts are often made of wood lashed together with cord."

Point out the illustration of a workbench on the Warm-Up Sheet. "This is a *workbench*. A workbench is a table where you can keep your tools and do small carpentry or electrical work, or repair small items."

"Have you ever had a favorite toy that was damaged or broken? What did you do to fix it?"

"The boy in this story has a damaged toy raft. Let's see if someone can fix it."

Read "Tin Raft"

"Turn to page 9 in your reader and read 'Tin Raft' aloud." Discuss your student's ideas for the questions below as you come to them.

After page 14: "Look at the raft in the illustration. Do you think it will be able to float now? Why or why not?"

After reading: "Why does Kent think this is the best gift?"

New Teaching
(continued)

Complete Activity Sheet

"Now let's read some of the words from the story and see if you can match them to the illustrations."

Make a Match
Remove pages 155-157 from the activity book.

Cut out the text and illustration cards.

Set the text cards in a pile face down. Spread the illustration cards face up on the table. Have your student draw one text card at a time, read it, and match it to the most appropriate illustration. If your student does not find the right match, return the card to the bottom of the stack to try again later.

Continue until your student has read all the text cards and matched them to the illustrations.

Story 2: "Lost in the Bog"

Read the Warm-Up Sheet for "Lost in the Bog"

Remove page 159 from the activity book.

Have your student practice reading words and phrases that will be encountered in "Lost in the Bog."

Point out the name *Sis* in the Names section. "Sis is a nickname for Sister."

Teach Vocabulary and Activate Prior Knowledge

Point out the illustration of an elf on the Warm-Up Sheet. "An *elf* is a small, imaginary human, often shown with pointy ears."

New Teaching
(continued)

Point out the illustration of a box turtle on the Warm-Up Sheet. "This is a *box turtle*. A box turtle is a land turtle with a low shell that can be completely closed around the animal inside. This type of turtle lives in North America and Mexico and is often kept as a pet."

"Have you ever seen a turtle? What do turtles do when they get scared? What do *you* do when you get scared?" Discuss how turtles hide in their shells, and what your student does when he is afraid of something.

"Let's see what happens when the turtle in this story gets scared."

Read "Lost in the Bog"

"Turn to page 19 in your reader and read 'Lost in the Bog' aloud." Discuss your student's ideas for the questions below as you come to them.

After page 22: "What do you think bumps Gump?"

After page 28: "Who do you think is on the path?"

Read-Aloud Time   Read a Story or Poem

Read aloud to your student for twenty minutes.

Track Your Progress   Mark the Progress Chart

Have your student mark Lesson 25 on the Progress Chart.

Lesson 26 - Words with Initial Blends

This lesson will teach words containing consonant blends at the beginning, as well as the Leap Word <u>to</u>.

You will need: ☐ *Blast Off to Reading!* pages 161-174

☐ Word Cards 113-122

Before You Begin

Preview Initial Blends

In this lesson, your student will learn to read words with consonant blends at the beginning. For most students, initial blends are slightly more difficult than final blends. Read the following examples and listen for the blends.

step   plan   swim   frog   glad

Don't Forget

Remember that a consonant blend is different from a consonant team. In consonant blends, each letter retains its own sound. In consonant teams, such as <u>th</u>, <u>sh</u>, and <u>ch</u>, two letters combine to make a completely new sound.

Review

Phonogram Cards

Review the Phonogram Cards that are behind the Review divider in your student's Reading Review Box. Show the card to your student and have him say the sound. If necessary, remind your student of the sound.

Word Cards

Review the Word Cards that are behind the Review divider in your student's Reading Review Box. If your student has difficulty reading the word, build the word with letter tiles and have your student sound it out using the procedure shown in Appendix C: Full Blending Procedure.

New Teaching

Blend Sounds with Letter Tiles

Build the word *spot* with letter tiles. | s | p | o | t |

"Sometimes there are two consonants at the beginning of a word, as in the word *spot*. Listen and watch as I blend the letters in this word: s-p-o-t."

Touch the s and say /s/. | s | p | o | t |

Touch the p and say /p/. | s | p | o | t |

Touch the o and say /ŏ/. | s | p | o | t |

Touch the t and say /t/. | s | p | o | t |

Now go back to the beginning of the word. Slide your finger under the letters s-p-o-t and say *spot* slowly.

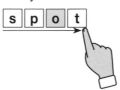

Finally, read the word *spot* at a normal pace, as we do when we speak.

Using the same procedure for blending, have your student sound out the word *flag*.

| f | l | a | g |

New Teaching
(continued)

Decode Words Containing Two-Letter Phonograms

Build the word *throb* with letter tiles. th r o b

"Sometimes one of the sounds at the beginning of a word is a consonant team, as in the word *throb*. Listen and watch as I blend the letters in this word: th-r-o-b."

Touch the th and say /th/.

Touch the r and say /r/.

Touch the o and say /ŏ/.

Touch the b and say /b/.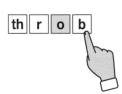

Now go back to the beginning of the word. Slide your finger under the letters th-r-o-b and say *throb* slowly.

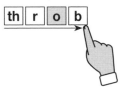

Finally, read the word *throb* at a normal pace, as we do when we speak.

Using the same procedure for blending, have your student sound out the word *shred*.

sh r e d

New Teaching
(continued)

Complete Activity Sheets

Word Flippers for Initial Blends
Remove pages 161-167 from the *Blast Off* activity book.

Refer to Appendix E for assembly instructions.

Have your student turn the pages and read the words that are formed.

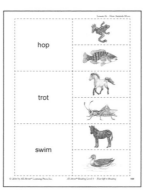

How Animals Move
Remove page 169 from the activity book.

Cut out the movement cards and the animal cards. Have your student match the picture of each animal with the movement it makes:

- *hop*   (frog, grasshopper)
- *trot*   (horse, zebra)
- *swim*   (fish, duck)

In some regions, *flag* is pronounced with a long a instead of a short a. If your student has difficulty reading the word *flag* due to pronunciation, make it a Leap Word, following the general format for the word *to* in the next section.

Practice Reading Words

Have your student practice reading the words on Word Cards 113-121.

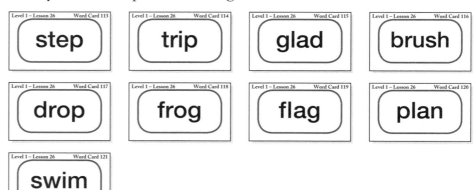

File the Word Cards behind the Review divider of the Reading Review Box.

Lesson 26: Words with Initial Blends

New Teaching
(continued)

We are treating the word *to* as a Leap Word because it contains the third sound of <u>o</u>, which has not been taught yet.

Teach a Leap Word: *to*

Show Word Card 122 to your student.

"This word is *to*, as in *Did you go to the lake?*"

Point to the <u>o</u>. "The <u>o</u> doesn't say the sound we expect it to."

Review this Leap Word several times today and then file it behind the Review divider in the Reading Review Box.

Practice Fluency

If you adapted the teaching of the word *flag* when you taught the Word Cards in this lesson, it is likely that you will need to adapt the words *drag, snag, stag,* and *brag* on this Practice Sheet as well.

Remove pages 171-174 from the activity book.

Have your student read from the Practice Sheet.

Read-Aloud Time   Read a Story or Poem

Read aloud to your student for twenty minutes.

Track Your Progress

Mark the Progress Chart

Have your student mark Lesson 26 on the Progress Chart.

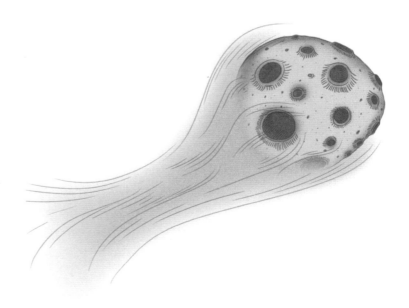

Lesson 26: Words with Initial Blends

Lesson 27 - Read "Lunch" and "The Big Top"

In this lesson, students will read two short stories and learn about onomatopoeia.

You will need: ☐ *Blast Off to Reading!* pages 175-178

☐ *The Runt Pig* book   ☐ Optional: *map or globe*

Before You Begin

Preview Onomatopoeia

Onomatopoeia is a word that imitates the natural sound of a particular thing. For example, the words *plop, plip, splash, drizzle, drip, sprinkle,* and *gush* are all onomatopoeic words that can describe water.

Onomatopoeia is pronounced /ŏn–ō–mah–tō–pē–uh/.

Here are some other common examples of onomatopoeia.

buzz	honk	quack
choo-choo	jingle	snarl
crash	oink	swish
ding dong	pitter patter	zoom

Review

Review the Phonogram Cards that are behind the Review divider in your student's Reading Review Box. Show the card to your student and have him say the sound(s). If necessary, remind your student of the sound(s).

Review the Word Cards that are behind the Review divider in your student's Reading Review Box. If your student has difficulty reading the word, build the word with letter tiles and have your student sound it out using the procedure shown in Appendix C: Full Blending Procedure.

New Teaching

Teach Onomatopoeia

"Some words imitate sound." Knock on a solid surface and say *knock knock*.

"You already know a lot of words that imitate sounds. What do cows say?" *Moo.*

"What do cats say?" *Meow* or *purr*.

"What do birds say?" *Tweet* or *chirp*.

"What does it sound like when a balloon breaks?" *Pop.*

Story 1: "Lunch"

Complete Activity Sheet

"Let's practice reading some words that imitate sounds."

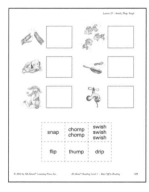

Swish and Flip!
Remove page 175 from the *Blast Off* activity book.

Cut out the word cards at the bottom of the page and spread them out on the table with the words facing up.

Have your student match each word with the drawing that makes that sound. For example, "chomp, chomp" should be matched with the drawing of the dog chomping on a bone.

Continue until all word cards have been matched to their illustrations.

Answer Key
twigs	*snap*
dog	*chomp, chomp*
rabbit	*thump*
fish	*swish, swish, swish*
pancakes	*flip*
faucet	*drip*

New Teaching
(continued)

Don't Forget

You will need the flip side of this Warm-Up Sheet for the next story, "The Big Top." If you won't be completing that portion of the lesson today, return this Warm-Up Sheet to the activity book for safekeeping.

Read the Warm-Up Sheet for "Lunch"

Remove page 177 from the activity book.

Have your student practice reading words and phrases that will be encountered in "Lunch."

Teach Vocabulary and Activate Prior Knowledge

Point out the illustration of a bunch of bananas on the Warm-Up Sheet. "A *bunch* is a number of things that are grouped or fastened together, like this bunch of bananas."

Point out the illustration of the fruit vendor on the Warm-Up Sheet. "This is a *fruit vendor*. A vendor is someone who sells something. This man sells bananas."

Find India on a map or globe. "This next story is set in India, a country in the southern part of Asia. Many vendors in India are experts at loading up their bicycles with their goods. This is how they transport their goods to the market. Do you think you could ride a bike loaded with bananas?"

"What is your favorite food? Pretend you live on a desert island, and your favorite food is dangling from a palm tree out of your reach. What are some ways you could try to get it?"

"In this next story, a chimp takes some chances to get his favorite food. Let's see what happens."

Read "Lunch"

"Turn to page 33 in your reader and read 'Lunch' aloud." Discuss your student's ideas for the questions below as you come to them.

After page 35: "How do you think the chimp will get the bananas from the bicycle?"

New Teaching
(continued)

After page 41: "How do you think this story will end? Will the chimp be happy or sad? Why?"

After reading: "This story uses a lot of onomatopoeia. Flip through the pages to find some examples." *Possible answers: swish, snap, thump, flop, chomp, gulp, munch.*

Story 2: "The Big Top"

Read the Warm-Up Sheet for "The Big Top"

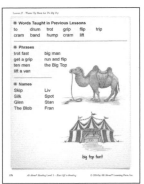

Remove page 178 from the activity book.

Have your student practice reading words and phrases that will be encountered in "The Big Top."

Teach Vocabulary and Activate Prior Knowledge

Point out the illustration of a big top tent on the Warm-Up Sheet. "This is a *big top tent*. The largest tent at a circus is called the *big top*, and many shows are held inside it."

Point out the illustration of a camel on the Warm-Up Sheet. "This is a *camel*. Camels are often included in circuses. Did you know that you can ride a camel? This camel has a fancy saddle."

Dromedary camels have one hump. Bactrian camels have two humps.

"Have you ever been to a circus? What kinds of things can you see at a circus?" Discuss the different people and animals at a circus, such as clowns, horses, elephants, and trapeze artists.

"The story you are going to read will explore many things you can see at a circus."

New Teaching
(continued)

Read "The Big Top"

"Turn to page 45 in your reader and read 'The Big Top' aloud." Discuss your student's answers for the questions below.

After reading: "Let's go back to look at some of the pictures. See if you can name some of the things found in a circus."

Page 47:	"What do we call this big tent?" *The big top.*
Page 51:	"Do you know what we call this swing?" *Trapeze.*
Page 52:	"Do you know what we call the person who works with the animals?" *Animal trainer, lion tamer.*
Page 53:	"What are these ten men?" *Clowns.*
Page 54:	"Do you know what we call a person who can lift heavy objects?" *The strong man.*
Page 55:	"What do we call a person who jumps and flips?" *Acrobat.*
Page 56:	"Do you know what we call the person who is in charge of the whole circus show?" *Ringmaster.*

Read-Aloud Time

Read a Story or Poem

Read aloud to your student for twenty minutes.

Track Your Progress

Mark the Progress Chart

Have your student mark Lesson 27 on the Progress Chart.

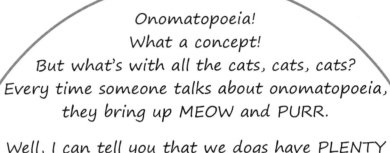

Onomatopoeia!
What a concept!
But what's with all the cats, cats, cats?
Every time someone talks about onomatopoeia,
they bring up MEOW and PURR.

Well, I can tell you that we dogs have PLENTY
of onomatopoeia of our own.
Try these on for size:

BARK
RUFF
ARF
WOOF
YIP
HOWL
WHINE
(I never do that, by the way.)

Take that, cats!

178

Lesson 28 - Read "Slim Went West" and "The Hit"

In this lesson, students will read two short stories that give them more practice with blends, and explore how objects can have multiple uses.

You will need: ☐ *Blast Off to Reading!* pages 179-182

☐ *The Runt Pig* book

Before You Begin

Provide Additional Practice with Initial Blends

In Lesson 26, your student learned how to decode words containing initial blends. As noted in that lesson, initial blends can be more difficult for students than final blends. For this reason, we've provided two extra stories to give your student additional practice with initial blends.

Your student may breeze right through these stories, or he may need extra time for decoding. The beauty of mastery-based lessons is that you can move at your student's individual pace.

Review

Review the Phonogram Cards that are behind the Review divider in your student's Reading Review Box. Show the card to your student and have him say the sound(s). If necessary, remind your student of the sound(s).

Review the Word Cards that are behind the Review divider in your student's Reading Review Box. If your student has difficulty reading the word, build the word with letter tiles and have your student sound it out using the procedure shown in Appendix C: Full Blending Procedure.

New Teaching

Complete Activity Sheet

"What are some of the different things you could do with a rubber band? A bed sheet?"

"In this activity, you'll look for many ways to use a single object."

What Could It Be?

Remove page 179 from the *Blast Off* activity book.

One at a time, have your student look at the four items. Your student should brainstorm as many ways as possible that the object could be used. For example, the hat could be used to keep cool on a hot day or to carry small objects. If you wish, write down your student's ideas.

Read the Warm-Up Sheet for "Slim Went West"

Don't Forget

You will need the flip side of this Warm-Up Sheet for the next story, "The Hit." If you won't be completing that portion of the lesson today, return this Warm-Up Sheet to the activity book for safe keeping.

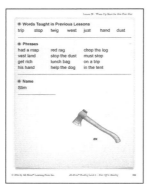

Remove page 181 from the activity book.

Have your student practice reading words and phrases that will be encountered in "Slim Went West."

Point out the name *Slim* in the Names section. "Slim is a nickname for someone who is tall and skinny."

Teach Vocabulary and Activate Prior Knowledge

Point out the illustration of an ax on the Warm-Up Sheet. "An *ax* is a tool for cutting wood. It has a heavy, sharp blade on the end of a wooden handle."

"The man in today's story uses an ax when he goes on an adventure to the vast Wild West. If something is *vast*, it is *very big*. Say the word with me: *vast*."

New Teaching
(continued)

"The *ocean* is vast. If you are in the middle of an ocean, it feels like it will go on and on forever. You can look in all directions, and all you can see is water. The *desert* is another vast place. You can look in all directions, and all you can see is sand."

"What is the opposite of *vast*?" *Possible answers: small, tiny, not large.*

"If you could go on a trip, where would you go?" Discuss where your student would go, and mention whether the destination is east, west, north, or south.

"Let's see what happens on this man's big adventure in the West."

Read "Slim Went West"

"Turn to page 59 in your reader and read 'Slim Went West' aloud." Discuss your student's ideas for the questions below as you come to them.

After page 62: "How do you think Slim will get rich in the West?"

After page 72: "Why do you think the items on this page make Slim rich?"

After reading: "What do you think Slim and his dog will do now? What would you do?"

"What different ways does Slim use the red rag?" Encourage your student to skim the story to find out.

Story 2: "The Hit"

Read the Warm-Up Sheet for "The Hit"

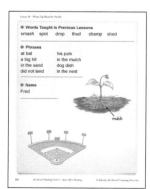

Remove page 182 from the activity book.

Have your student practice reading words and phrases that will be encountered in "The Hit."

Teach Vocabulary and Activate Prior Knowledge

Point out the illustration of mulch on the Warm-Up Sheet. "A material made of decaying leaves, bark, or compost is called *mulch*. Mulch is spread around plants to enrich the soil and protect the plants."

Point out the illustration of a baseball diamond on the Warm-Up Sheet. "This is a *baseball diamond*. A baseball diamond is the field where you play baseball. The four bases on the field are placed in the shape of a diamond, with the pitcher's mound in the middle."

"Have you ever lost something you really liked? Where did you look for it? Did you ever find it?" Discuss your student's lost item and if and how he found it.

"Let's see what happens when the boys in this story lose their baseball."

Read "The Hit"

"Turn to page 75 in your reader and read 'The Hit' aloud." Discuss your student's ideas for the questions below as you come to them.

After page 80: "Do you think the boys will find the ball?"

After pages 85: "The boys have looked everywhere. Where do you think the ball could be?"

Read-Aloud Time

Read a Story or Poem

Read aloud to your student for twenty minutes.

**Track Your
Progress**

Mark the Progress Chart

Have your student mark Lesson 28 on the Progress Chart.

Lesson 28: Read "Slim Went West" and "The Hit"

Lesson 29 - FF, LL, and SS

This lesson will teach words ending in <u>ff</u>, <u>ll</u>, and <u>ss</u>, as well as the Leap Words <u>said</u> and <u>I</u>.

You will need: ☐ *Blast Off to Reading!* pages 183-195

☐ Extra <u>f</u>, <u>l</u>, and <u>s</u> letter tiles

☐ Word Cards 123-132

Before You Begin

In the *All About Spelling* series, we call this pattern the Floss Rule because the word *floss* follows the rule and contains the letters <u>f</u>, <u>l</u>, and <u>s</u>. In spelling, your student will learn that these letters are often doubled after a single vowel at the end of a one-syllable word, and he will learn the exceptions to this pattern. This information isn't needed for reading purposes, however.

Preview Words Ending in FF, LL, and SS

The letters <u>f</u>, <u>l</u>, and <u>s</u> are doubled at the end of approximately one hundred common one-syllable words, as in the examples below.

ff:	cliff	fluff	staff
ll:	well	still	smell
ss:	miss	dress	glass

Occasionally other consonants are doubled at the end of one-syllable words, too, such as <u>z</u> (*buzz, fizz*), <u>n</u> (*inn, Ann*), <u>d</u> (*add, odd*) and <u>g</u> (*egg*), although not as regularly.

In this lesson, your student will learn that when a doubled consonant appears at the end of a word, he only has to pronounce one of them.

Organize the Extra Letter Tiles

You will need extra <u>f</u>, <u>l</u>, and <u>s</u> tiles for this lesson. Place them on the board as follows.

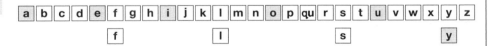

Preview Direct Quotations

The word *said* is used quite often in books in which there is a lot of dialogue. Consider these examples:
- My brother said, "The turtle bit me!"
- "I told you to keep your fingers out of his cage!" said Mom.

When we talk, we normally use the noun-verb pattern, as in *Frank said,*

"Let's eat." But in books, it tends to be the opposite. Authors usually use the verb-noun pattern, as in *"Let's eat," said Frank.*

Because you have been reading aloud to your student every day, he should be used to hearing this verb-noun pattern. Today's Practice Sheet will give your student practice with reading direct quotations.

Review

Review the Phonogram Cards that are behind the Review divider in your student's Reading Review Box. Show the card to your student and have him say the sound. If necessary, remind your student of the sound.

Review the Word Cards that are behind the Review divider in your student's Reading Review Box. If your student has difficulty reading the word, build the word with letter tiles and have your student sound it out using the procedure shown in Appendix C: Full Blending Procedure.

New Teaching

Blend Sounds with Letter Tiles

Build the word *stiff* with letter tiles. | s | t | i | f | f |

"I'll sound out this first word, and then you'll sound out the next word."

Touch the s̲ and say /s/.
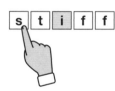

Touch the t̲ and say /t/.

Touch the i̲ and say /ĭ/.
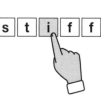

New Teaching
(continued)

Touch the two f's and say /f/.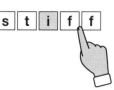

"Notice that there are two f's here. I only have to pronounce one of them."

Now go back to the beginning of the word. Slide your finger under the letters s-t-i-f-f and say *stiff* slowly.

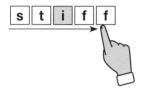

Finally, read the word *stiff* at a normal pace, as we do when we speak.

"When we see two of the same letter at the end of a word, we only pronounce it once. We wouldn't say *stiff-ff* because that would sound funny."

Using the same procedure for blending, have your student sound out the words *glass* and *bill*.

Complete Activity Sheets

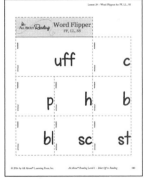

Word Flippers for FF, LL, and SS
Remove pages 183-187 from the *Blast Off* activity book.

Refer to Appendix E for assembly instructions.

Have your student turn the pages and read the words that are formed.

New Teaching
(continued)

On the Trail
Remove pages 189-192 from the activity book.

Cut out the sixteen game cards on page 191 and place one on each square of the game board with the words facing down.

"Frisky Fox is chasing a dragonfly. Follow Frisky to see what she sees."

Have your student follow the path of the cards to reach the dragonfly by turning the cards over one by one and reading the words aloud.

Practice Reading Words

Have your student practice reading the words on Word Cards 123-130.

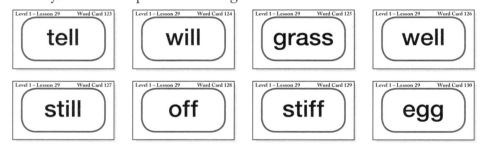

File the Word Cards behind the Review divider of the Reading Review Box.

Teach Two Leap Words: *said* and *I*

Show Word Card 131 to your student.

"Most words follow the rules and say the sounds that we expect them to say. But there are a few words that do not. Here is one of those words."

"This word is *said*, as in *She said hello*."

Lesson 29: FF, LL, and SS

New Teaching

(continued)

Show Word Card 132 to your student.

"This word is *I*, as in *I am a student*. The word *I* is always spelled with a capital i."

Review these Leap Words several times today and then file them behind the Review divider in the Reading Review Box.

We are treating the word *I* as a Leap Word because it contains the long sound of i, which has not been taught yet.

Practice Fluency

Remove pages 193-195 from the activity book.

Have your student read from the Practice Sheet.

Read-Aloud Time Read a Story or Poem

Read aloud to your student for twenty minutes.

Track Your Progress Mark the Progress Chart

Have your student mark Lesson 29 on the Progress Chart.

Lesson 29: FF, LL, and SS

Lesson 30 - Read "Mud Milk" and "The Ant Hill"

In this lesson, students will read two short stories and follow recipe instructions.

You will need: ☐ *Blast Off to Reading!* pages 197-202

☐ *The Runt Pig* book

Emma 12/31 1/2

Review

Review the Phonogram Cards that are behind the Review divider in your student's Reading Review Box. Show the card to your student and have him say the sound(s). If necessary, remind your student of the sound(s).

Review the Word Cards that are behind the Review divider in your student's Reading Review Box. If your student has difficulty reading the word, build the word with letter tiles and have your student sound it out using the procedure shown in Appendix C: Full Blending Procedure.

Shuffle the cards behind the **Mastered** dividers and choose a selection for review.

As always, if your student has any difficulty reading the stories, review the Practice Sheets of the previous lessons. Refer to Appendix J for more tips.

New Teaching

Complete Activity Sheet

"Have you ever used a recipe? In this activity, you'll follow a recipe to make a pie for a pig."

Pie for a Pig

Remove pages 197-200 from the *Blast Off* activity book.

Cut out the pie tin on page 197. Cut out the ingredient cards and spoon along the dotted lines shown on page 200.

Place the pie tin in front of your student and spread the ingredient cards above it. Tell your student that she is going to make a pie for a pig by listening to your recipe directions. With each direction, your student will put the proper ingredient in the pie tin.

Continue until your student has finished her pie for a pig.

Recipe directions

1. Put the potato peelings in the pie dish.
2. Put the cheese under the potato peelings.
3. Put the carrot tops over the potato peelings.
4. Sprinkle the bread crumbs over the whole pie.
5. Use the wooden spoon to pat down all the ingredients.
6. Carefully fold the top pie crust over all the ingredients.
7. Feed the pie to your pig!

New Teaching
(continued)

Don't Forget

You will need the flip side of this Warm-Up Sheet for the next story, "The Ant Hill." If you won't be completing that portion of the lesson today, return this Warm-Up Sheet to the activity book for safekeeping.

Read the Warm-Up Sheet for "Mud Milk"

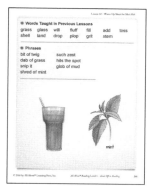

Remove page 201 from the activity book.

Have your student practice reading words and phrases that will be encountered in "Mud Milk."

Teach Vocabulary and Activate Prior Knowledge

Point out the illustration of mint on the Warm-Up Sheet. "*Mint* is a plant with leaves that have a strong, fresh taste. You have probably tasted mint in candies or even toothpaste."

Point out the illustration of a milkshake on the Warm-Up Sheet. "And there are even mint *milkshakes*! What is your favorite drink when you are thirsty?"

"Sometimes when people like the taste of something, they say it *really hits the spot*. Let's see what hits the spot for the girl in this story."

Read "Mud Milk"

"Turn to page 89 in your reader and read 'Mud Milk' aloud." Discuss your student's ideas for the questions below as you come to them.

After reading: "Did you notice that this story rhymes? Let's look at it again and see if we can find the rhyming words." *Possible answers: grass/ glass, sand/land, bud/mud, zest/best, grit/fit, top/plop.*

"Do you think the girl is really going to drink her mud milk? Would you?"

New Teaching
(continued)

Read the Warm-Up Sheet for "The Ant Hill"

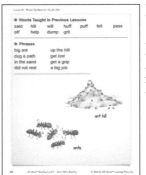

Remove page 202 from the activity book.

Have your student practice reading words and phrases that will be encountered in "The Ant Hill."

Teach Vocabulary and Activate Prior Knowledge

Point out the illustration of an ant hill on the Warm-Up Sheet. "An *ant hill* is the mound of dirt or sand that ants throw to the surface as they dig their tunnels underground."

Point out the word *ants* under the illustration of the ants. Cover up the s with your finger. "What is this word?" *Ant.*

Uncover the s to reveal the full word *ants*. "When we add an s to the word, we get *ants*."

"Have you ever observed ants working on an ant hill? They are very busy, aren't they? What do you see ants do as they work?" Discuss how ants climb and carry bits of dirt and grass.

"The ants in the next story work very hard. Let's see what they are building."

Lesson 30: Read "Mud Milk" and "The Ant Hill"

New Teaching
(continued)

Read "The Ant Hill"

"Turn to page 97 in your reader and read 'The Ant Hill' aloud." Discuss your student's ideas for the questions below as you come to them.

After page 100: "What do you think the ants are building?"

After page 101: "What keeps the ants from getting lost?" *Possible answers: Their antennae, sticking together as they work, the scent trail of other ants.*

After page 105: "The ants work hard for a long time. Why do you think they need such a big hill?"

After page 106: "Sometimes authors like to surprise their readers. Are you surprised by what the ants built?"

Read-Aloud Time

Read a Story or Poem

Read aloud to your student for twenty minutes.

Track Your Progress

Mark the Progress Chart

Have your student mark Lesson 30 on the Progress Chart.

You know,
that pig pie didn't sound half bad.
Did you try some?
Was it paw-licking good?

Can you guess what <u>my</u> favorite pie is?

MOON PIE, of course!

Graham crackers, chocolate, marshmallow ... mmm.
If you'll excuse me, I have to run to the space store
to stock up before our next blastoff!

We have some phonogram showers
coming our way and will need fortifications!

YUM!

194

Lesson 30: Read "Mud Milk" and "The Ant Hill"

Lesson 31 - Three Leap Words

This lesson will teach the Leap Words <u>or</u>, <u>for</u>, and <u>no</u>.

You will need: ☐ *Blast Off to Reading!* pages 203-206

☐ Word Cards 133-135

Emma 1/4

Before You Begin

Preview Leap Words

Today's lesson is a relatively short one. Your student will learn three Leap Words: *or, for,* and *no*. If your student learns these words quickly, you may wish to continue on to the stories in Lesson 32 or expand your read-aloud time.

The first two Leap Words include phonogram <u>or</u>. The words *or* and *for* are common words that should be introduced at this stage, although phonogram <u>or</u> won't be taught until Level 2, Lesson 35.

Review

Review the Phonogram Cards that are behind the Review divider in your student's Reading Review Box. Show the card to your student and have him say the sound. If necessary, remind your student of the sound.

Review the Word Cards that are behind the Review divider in your student's Reading Review Box. If your student has difficulty reading the word, build the word with letter tiles and have your student sound it out using the procedure shown in Appendix C: Full Blending Procedure.

New Teaching

Teach Three Leap Words: *or, for,* and *no*

"Today we have three words that don't say what we expect them to say."

Show Word Card 133 to your student.

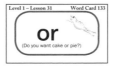

"This word is *or*, as in *Do you want cake or pie?*"

Show Word Card 134 to your student.

"This word is *for*, as in *I have a surprise for you.*"

Show Word Card 135 to your student.

"This word is *no*, as in *There are no more cookies.*"

Review these Leap Words several times today and then file them behind the Review divider in the Reading Review Box.

> We are treating *or* and *for* as Leap Words because they contain the phonogram or, which has not been taught yet.
>
> The word *no* is also treated as a Leap Word at this stage because long vowels have not been taught yet.

Complete Activity Sheet

Who Is It For?

Remove page 203 from the *Blast Off* activity book.

Cut out the three child cards at the top of the page and the three gift cards at the bottom of the page.

Have your student match each gift card to the appropriate child by reading and verbally answering the three questions. Your student should refer to the gift cards for answers.

New Teaching
(continued)

Practice Fluency

Remove pages 205-206 from the activity book.

Have your student read from the Practice Sheet.

Vocabulary Affects Fluency

Tip!

If you've ever picked up a book outside of your expertise (such as a medical book if you are an architect, or an engineering book if you are a horticulturist), then you've encountered unfamiliar vocabulary words that you don't understand. It would be difficult for you to read these books fluently because you wouldn't know how to pronounce many of the words. In the same way, it is difficult for your student to read fluently if he doesn't understand what the words mean.

You can help your student develop a large listening vocabulary by reading aloud from a wide variety of books and discussing unfamiliar words.

Read-Aloud Time   Read a Story or Poem

Read aloud to your student for twenty minutes.

Track Your Progress

Mark the Progress Chart

Have your student mark Lesson 31 on the Progress Chart.

Lesson 31: Three Leap Words

Lesson 32 - Read "The Plan" and "The Big Mess"

In this lesson, students will read two short stories that give them more practice with previously taught concepts.

You will need: ☐ *Blast Off to Reading!* pages 207-210

☐ *The Runt Pig* book

Emma 1/7

Review

Review the Phonogram Cards that are behind the Review divider in your student's Reading Review Box. Show the card to your student and have him say the sound(s). If necessary, remind your student of the sound(s).

Review the Word Cards that are behind the Review divider in your student's Reading Review Box. If your student has difficulty reading the word, build the word with letter tiles and have your student sound it out using the procedure shown in Appendix C: Full Blending Procedure.

If your student has any difficulty reading the next two stories, review the Practice Sheets of the previous lessons.

New Teaching

Story 1: "The Plan"

Complete Activity Sheet

"Lots of people like to use old clothes and blankets to create new items. In this activity, you'll create something new out of something old."

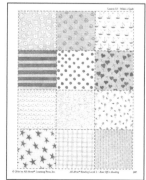

Make a Quilt
Remove pages 207-208 from the *Blast Off* activity book.

Cut out the quilt squares on page 207.

Mix up the cards and place them in a pile with the illustrations of the shorts, shirts, sundresses, and pants facing up. Have your student turn the cards

New Teaching
(continued)

over one by one to reveal a close-up of the pattern on the item. Your student should arrange the cards in a pattern to create a quilt.

Read the Warm-Up Sheet for "The Plan"

Don't Forget

You will need the flip side of this Warm-Up Sheet for the next story, "The Big Mess." If you won't be completing that portion of the lesson today, return this Warm-Up Sheet to the activity book for safekeeping.

Remove page 209 from the activity book.

Have your student practice reading words and phrases that will be encountered in "The Plan."

Teach Vocabulary and Activate Prior Knowledge

Point out the illustration of silk on the Warm-Up Sheet. "*Silk* is a strong, soft fiber used to make thread and fabric. It is produced by silkworms when they make their cocoons."

"Do you have a favorite blanket or pillow? Why do you like it so much?" Discuss where your student got the favorite item and why it's so special.

"What do you call your grandmother? Some families use different names, like Grandma or Nana. In this story, the girl calls her grandmother *Gram*. She receives a wonderful gift from Gram, too. Let's see what it is!"

Read "The Plan"

"Turn to page 109 in your reader and read 'The Plan' aloud." Discuss your student's ideas for the questions below as you come to them.

After page 114: "What do you think Gram is making?"

After reading: "Which items does Gram cut up to make the quilt? Skim the story to find out."

New Teaching
(continued)

Read the Warm-Up Sheet for "The Big Mess"

Remove page 210 from the activity book.

Have your student practice reading words and phrases that will be encountered in "The Big Mess."

Teach Vocabulary and Activate Prior Knowledge

Point out the illustration of a mix on the Warm-Up Sheet. "A box of prepared ingredients is called a *mix*. You can use a mix to make brownies, cakes, pancakes, and other goodies."

Point out the illustration of pancakes on the Warm-Up Sheet. "A *pancake* is a thin, flat cake made of batter that is fried on both sides in a pan. Another name for pancakes is *flapjacks*. Many people eat pancakes with maple syrup, butter, or jam."

"Do you like to cook and bake? What kinds of things do you like to make?" Discuss your student's experiences in the kitchen.

"The boy in this story likes to make pancakes. Let's see what happens."

Read "The Big Mess"

"Turn to page 119 in your reader and read 'The Big Mess' aloud." Discuss your student's ideas for the question below when you come to it.

After reading: "What ingredients does Chen use to make the pancakes? Skim the story to find out."

Read-Aloud Time   Read a Story or Poem

Read aloud to your student for twenty minutes.

Track Your Progress

Mark the Progress Chart

Have your student mark Lesson 32 on the Progress Chart.

Lesson 32: Read "The Plan" and "The Big Mess"

Lesson 33 - Read "The Runt Pig" and "Fish Class"

In this lesson, students will read two short stories that give them more practice with previously taught concepts, and learn about main conflicts in stories.

You will need: ☐ *Blast Off to Reading!* pages 211-214

☐ *The Runt Pig* book

Emma 1/11

Review

Review the Phonogram Cards that are behind the Review divider in your student's Reading Review Box. Show the card to your student and have him say the sound(s). If necessary, remind your student of the sound(s).

Review the Word Cards that are behind the Review divider in your student's Reading Review Box. If your student has difficulty reading the word, build the word with letter tiles and have your student sound it out using the procedure shown in Appendix C: Full Blending Procedure.

If you are using *Reading Games with Ziggy the Zebra*, you can play "Ziggy Rounds Up Horses" for an engaging way to review Phonogram Cards and Word Cards.

If your student has any difficulty reading the next two stories, review the Practice Sheets of the previous lessons.

New Teaching

Complete Activity Sheet

"In this activity, you'll find solutions to various problems."

<u>**Can You Solve It?**</u>
Remove pages 211-212 from the *Blast Off* activity book.

Cut out the cards on the left side of the page (the "problems," which have a P on the back) and place them face down in a stack. Cut out the cards on the right side of the page (the "solutions," which have an S on the back) and arrange them on the table with the solutions facing up.

Have your student select a "problem" card and read it aloud. Then have him select an appropriate "solution" card to solve the problem. Discuss your student's choices.

Continue until all the problems have been solved.

Read the Warm-Up Sheet for "The Runt Pig"

Don't Forget You will need the flip side of this Warm-Up Sheet for the next story, "Fish Class." If you won't be completing that portion of the lesson today, return this Warm-Up Sheet to the activity book for safekeeping.

Remove page 213 from the activity book.

Have your student practice reading words and phrases that will be encountered in "The Runt Pig."

Teach Vocabulary and Activate Prior Knowledge

This discussion introduces the idiomatic expression *to lend a hand*. An idiomatic expression, or idiom, is a phrase whose meaning is different from that of the literal words that make it up.

You may wish to point out idiomatic expressions as your student comes across them in other stories or in everyday conversation.

Point out the illustration of a ramp on the Warm-Up Sheet. "A *ramp* is a sloping platform that connects two different levels. Ramps are often used instead of stairs to make it easier to push heavy objects from one level to another, or to help people in wheelchairs."

Point out the illustration of a runt on the Warm-Up Sheet. "This kitten is a *runt*. That means she is the smallest kitten in the litter. Other animals can be runts, too, such as puppies, pigs, or chipmunks."

"Has a friend or relative ever needed your help with something? How did you feel after you helped this person?" Discuss your student's experience.

"When you help someone, we say that you *lend them a hand*. It's just an expression. You don't really give them one of your hands!"

"In the next story, a runt pig lends a hand to his fellow animals on the farm. Let's see what happens."

Read "The Runt Pig"

"Turn to page 131 in your reader and read 'The Runt Pig' aloud." Discuss your student's ideas for the questions below as you come to them.

After page 133: "Do you think Bret likes being a runt pig? Why or why not?"

After page 143: "Do you think Bret will be able to help the hen? How?"

After page 148: "Bret is sad at the beginning of the story. How do you think he feels now? Why?"

Discuss the Main Conflict

"In a story, the problem that a character faces is called the *conflict*. What do you think is the biggest conflict in this story?" Encourage your student to skim the text for clues if necessary.

"What does Bret do to solve the problem?"

"Why is Bret the only character who is able to solve the problem?"

Story 2: "Fish Class"

Read the Warm-Up Sheet for "Fish Class"

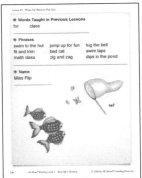

Remove page 214 from the activity book.

Have your student practice reading words and phrases that will be encountered in "Fish Class."

Teach Vocabulary and Activate Prior Knowledge

Point out the illustration of a net on the Warm-Up Sheet. "A *net* is a type of open bag made of strong cord. It is used for catching fish or butterflies."

Point to the illustration of a school of fish. "Many fish travel in large groups like this. The group is called a *school of fish*. The fish stay together for protection from bigger fish and other animals that might eat them."

"This next story is about a school of fish, but not this type of school! Let's find out what kind of school it is."

Read "Fish Class"

"Turn to page 151 in your reader and read 'Fish Class' aloud." Discuss your student's ideas for the questions below as you come to them.

After page 155: "Why is class #2 important for the fish?"

After reading: "Look at all the classes again. Which class do you think is the most important for these fish? Which one is the least important? Why?"

Read-Aloud Time   Read a Story or Poem

Read aloud to your student for twenty minutes.

Track Your Progress

Mark the Progress Chart

Have your student mark Lesson 33 on the Progress Chart.

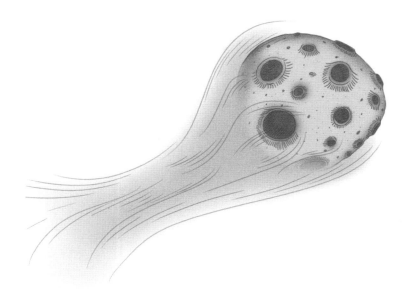

Wow, four stories in a row!
Now I need a new book for nap time
in the rocket. Any suggestions?

You probably didn't know that dogs are big readers,
but we are! I like stories about simple things like
tail-chasing, as well as big tales of space adventure.

The best thing about reading is all the people I meet
and places I go in the stories. The other day a
spaceship full of rookie pilots almost crashed into a
satellite. Lucky for them that Rocket the Dog was
there to save their hides!

What have you been reading during
Read-Aloud Time?

Lesson 33: Read "The Runt Pig" and "Fish Class"

Lesson 34 - Consonant Team CK

This lesson will teach words containing the consonant team <u>ck</u>.

You will need: ☐ Phonogram Card 30   ☐ *Blast Off to Reading!* pages 215-229
☐ Letter tile <u>ck</u>   ☐ Word Cards 136-145

Emma 1/14

Before You Begin

Preview Consonant Team CK

ck The consonant team <u>ck</u> says /k/ as in *duck*. It is typically found immediately after a short vowel.

Listen to the *Phonogram Sounds* app for a demonstration of the phonogram sounds.

Store the new tile under the following label:

Consonant Teams

ck

Review

Phonogram Cards

Review the Phonogram Cards that are behind the Review divider in your student's Reading Review Box. Show the card to your student and have him say the sound. If necessary, remind your student of the sound.

Word Cards

Review the Word Cards that are behind the Review divider in your student's Reading Review Box. If your student has difficulty reading the word, build the word with letter tiles and have your student sound it out using the procedure shown in Appendix C: Full Blending Procedure.

New Teaching

Teach New Letter Sounds

"Point to the letter tiles that can say /k/." *Student points to the c and k tiles.*

"Today you will learn another letter tile that can say /k/." Set out the ck tile.

"The c and k work together to say one sound: /k/."

Teach the Phonogram Card for the consonant team ck.

Level 1 – Lesson 34 Phonogram Card 30
ck

1. Hold up the Phonogram Card and demonstrate the sound.
2. Have your student repeat the sound.

Mix in several other Phonogram Cards for mixed review and practice until your student can say the sounds accurately. File the new Phonogram Card behind the Review divider in the Reading Review Box.

Mix in several other letter tiles for mixed review and practice with the new tile until your student can say the sound accurately.

Blend Sounds with Letter Tiles

Build the word *pick* with letter tiles. | p | i | ck |

"I'll sound out this first word, and then you'll sound out the next word."

Touch the p and say /p/.

Touch the i and say /ĭ/.

Touch the ck and say /k/.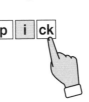

Lesson 34: Consonant Team CK

New Teaching
(continued)

Now go back to the beginning of the word. Slide your finger under the letters p-i-ck and say *pick* slowly.

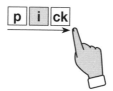

Finally, read the word *pick* at a normal pace, as we do when we speak.

Using the same procedure for blending, have your student sound out the word *neck*.

Play "Change the Word"

Build the word *snack*. | s | n | a | ck |

"What is this word?" *Snack.*

"I'm going to change the second letter of this word."

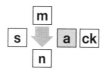

"What does this new word say?" Encourage your student to sound out the new word. *Smack.*

Continue to change one letter at a time to form the following words. Each time, have your student sound out the new word.

smack → sack → sick → pick → lick → luck → pluck

New Teaching
(continued)

Complete Activity Sheets

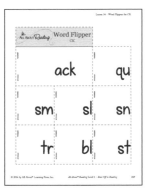

Word Flippers for CK

Remove pages 215-221 from the *Blast Off* activity book.

Refer to Appendix E for assembly instructions.

Have your student turn the pages and read the words that are formed.

A Flock of Ducks

Remove pages 223-225 from the activity book.

Have your student color the pond and ducks, if desired. Cut out the ducks.

Place the adult duck cards in a pile and arrange the baby duck cards in the pond. Have your student select an adult duck card and read the word aloud. Then choose a baby duck card and read the word aloud. If he reads the word correctly, reunite the baby duck with its parent. If he reads the word incorrectly, return the baby duck to the pond for another try.

Optional: Match up the rhyming pairs of adult and baby duck cards.

Continue until all the ducks have been reunited with their babies.

New Teaching
(continued)

Practice Reading Words

Have your student practice reading the words on Word Cards 136-145.

File the Word Cards behind the Review divider of the Reading Review Box.

Practice Fluency

Remove pages 227-229 from the activity book.

Have your student read from the Practice Sheet.

Read-Aloud Time   Read a Story or Poem

Read aloud to your student for twenty minutes.

Track Your Progress

Mark the Progress Chart

Have your student mark Lesson 34 on the Progress Chart.

Lesson 34: Consonant Team CK

Lesson 35 - Read "The Pet Duck" and "Fun at the Pond"

In this lesson, students will read two short stories that give them practice with words containing <u>ck</u>, and learn about character traits.

You will need: ☐ *Blast Off to Reading!* pages 231-237

☐ *The Runt Pig* book

Elijah 12/3

Before You Begin

Preview Character Traits

In today's activity, your student will discuss the character traits of the duck in the first story. Character traits are the way that a person or animal is, such as friendly, selfish, or naughty. A person can have many traits.

Review

Review the Phonogram Cards that are behind the Review divider in your student's Reading Review Box. Show the card to your student and have him say the sound(s). If necessary, remind your student of the sound(s).

Review the Word Cards that are behind the Review divider in your student's Reading Review Box. If your student has difficulty reading the word, build the word with letter tiles and have your student sound it out using the procedure shown in Appendix C: Full Blending Procedure.

New Teaching

Story 1: "The Pet Duck"

Read the Warm-Up Sheet for "The Pet Duck"

Remove page 231 from the *Blast Off* activity book.

Have your student practice reading words and phrases that will be encountered in "The Pet Duck."

New Teaching
(continued)

Teach Vocabulary and Activate Prior Knowledge

Point out the illustration of a bill on the Warm-Up Sheet. "*Bill* is another word for the beak of a bird. The bird in this illustration is a woodpecker. It uses its long bill as a chisel to remove tree bark and find insects."

Point out the illustration of a top hat on the Warm-Up Sheet. "This is a *top hat*. Top hats are usually black and have a high cylindrical crown. Abraham Lincoln was famous for wearing a top hat. Nowadays top hats are worn only when gentlemen dress up for formal occasions."

"The little girl in the next story has a pet duck that wears a top hat. Let's see what this duck does."

Read "The Pet Duck"

"Turn to page 163 in your reader and read 'The Pet Duck' aloud." Discuss your student's ideas for the questions below as you come to them.

After page 173: "What does *six on the dot* mean?"

After reading: "Rick is quite a naughty duck. What kind of trouble does he get into? Skim the story to find out."

"Even though Rick is naughty, Quinn thinks he is the best pet. Why?"

Complete Activity Sheet

"The way that a person or even an animal is—such as friendly, selfish, or naughty—is called a *character trait*. A person can have many traits. In this activity, you'll discover the character traits of the pet duck."

What Is Rick Like?
Remove pages 233-236 from the activity book.

Cut out the word cards on page 235.

Mix up the cards and place them in a pile with the illustrations facing up. Have your student turn the cards over one by one, read the word, and decide whether that word describes Rick the duck. If it

Lesson 35: Read "The Pet Duck" and "Fun at the Pond"

New Teaching
(continued)

does, the student should set the card on top of the illustration of Rick. If it does not, the student should set the card aside.

If your student puts a word on Rick that does not describe the character, allow him to defend his choice. More advanced readers may understand the explanation that nothing in the text supports that idea, but younger readers may tend to put their own feelings onto the duck. Ask your student to explain his answers, and then accept them at this early stage.

Words that describe Rick	Words that do not describe Rick
fun	sad
bad	hot
fast	rich
mad	stuck
glad	lost
quick	thin

Story 2: "Fun at the Pond"

Read the Warm-Up Sheet for "Fun at the Pond"

Remove page 237 from the activity book.

Have your student practice reading words and phrases that will be encountered in "Fun at the Pond."

Teach Vocabulary and Activate Prior Knowledge

Point out the illustration of a lily pad on the Warm-Up Sheet. "A *pad*, or lily pad, is the large, floating leaf of the water lily plant. These plants grow in the water of a pond or pool, and frogs like to sit on them to bask in the sun. The word *bask* means to relax in the warmth of the sun. That's what frogs do on lily pads!"

New Teaching
(continued)

"Have you ever been to a pond? What things can you see at a pond?" *Possible answers: frogs, lily pads, cattails, fish, water, birds, sand, butterflies.*

Point to the illustration of a crayfish. "Sometimes you might even see a *crayfish* at a pond. In some areas, these are called *crawfish* or *crawdads*. Crayfish resemble small lobsters and live in streams and rivers."

"In the next story, three children have lots of fun at the pond. Let's see what they find there."

Read "Fun at the Pond"

"Turn to page 179 in your reader and read 'Fun at the Pond' aloud." Discuss your student's ideas for the questions below as you come to them.

After page 192: "Do you think the kids will catch a fish?"

After reading: "What kinds of animals do the children meet at the pond? Skim the story to find out."

Read-Aloud Time

Read a Story or Poem

Read aloud to your student for twenty minutes.

Track Your Progress

Mark the Progress Chart

Have your student mark Lesson 35 on the Progress Chart.

Lesson 35: Read "The Pet Duck" and "Fun at the Pond"

Lesson 36 - Consonant Team NG

This lesson will teach words containing the consonant team ng.

You will need: ☐ Phonogram Card 31   ☐ Blast Off to Reading! pages 239-247
☐ Letter tile ng   ☐ Word Cards 146-155

Elijah 1/2

Before You Begin

Preview Consonant Team NG

ng The consonant team ng says /ng/ as in *ring*. Listen for the /ng/ sound in the following words.

sing   rang   long   bring   thing

When phonogram ng comes after a and i, the vowels don't say their pure short vowel sound. Instead, the sound falls between the short and long vowel sound, as in the words *sang* and *thing*.

This concept is generally easy for students to grasp, since it is difficult to say the pure short vowel sound in these word parts. It is easier to say the word parts correctly.

Less commonly, ng combines with e to form the word part *eng*, as in *English* and *strength*. There are only a few words with the *eng* word part, and since none of them appear at this reading level, words containing *eng* have not been included in this lesson.

Listen to the *Phonogram Sounds* app for a demonstration of the phonogram sounds.

Store the new tile under the following label:

Consonant Teams

ng

Review

Review the Phonogram Cards that are behind the Review divider in your student's Reading Review Box. Show the card to your student and have him say the sound. If necessary, remind your student of the sound.

Review the Word Cards that are behind the Review divider in your student's Reading Review Box. If your student has difficulty reading the word, build the word with letter tiles and have your student sound it out using the procedure shown in Appendix C: Full Blending Procedure.

New Teaching

Teach New Letter Sounds

Teach the Phonogram Card for the consonant team <u>ng</u>.

1. Hold up the Phonogram Card and demonstrate the sound.
2. Have your student repeat the sound.

Mix in several other Phonogram Cards for mixed review and practice until your student can say the sounds accurately. File the new Phonogram Card behind the Review divider in the Reading Review Box.

Set out the new letter tile. ng

Mix in several other letter tiles for mixed review and practice with the new tile until your student can say the sound accurately.

Blend Sounds with Letter Tiles

Build the word part *ang* with letter tiles. a ng

"This word part says /ang/. Let's make some words with /ang/."

One at a time, build the words *bang, fang, hang,* and *rang*, and read them with your student.

Build the word part *ing*. i ng

Lesson 36: Consonant Team NG

New Teaching
(continued)

"This word part says /ing/."

One at a time, build the words *sing, king, ring, thing,* and *wing* and read them with your student.

Build the word part *ong*.   o ng

"<u>Ng</u> can be combined with <u>o</u>, too. The <u>o</u> says /ŏ/ just like we expect it to say."

One at a time, build the words *song, long,* and *gong* and read them with your student.

Build the word part *ung*.   u ng

"And <u>ng</u> can be combined with <u>u</u>. The <u>u</u> says /ŭ/ just like we expect it to say."

One at a time, build the words *hung, sung, flung,* and *lung* and read them with your student.

h u ng   s u ng   f l u ng   l u ng

Arrange the letter tiles as follows.

Point to the *ang* word part. "Say this word part." *Ang.*

Move the <u>ng</u> down to form the *ing* word part. "Say this word part." *Ing.*

Repeat with the remaining vowels, and then do mixed review until your student can easily read all four word parts.

New Teaching
(continued)

Play "Change the Word"

Build the word *thing*.

"What is this word?" *Thing.*

"I'm going to change the first letter of this word."

"What does this new word say?" Encourage your student to sound out the new word. *Ring.*

Continue to change one letter at a time to form the following words. Each time, have your student sound out the new word.

ring → rang → sang → sing → song → sung → stung → sting

Complete Activity Sheets

Matching Mittens
Remove pages 239-240 from the *Blast Off* activity book.

Cut out the kitten and all the mittens.

Lay the mittens on a table with the words facing down and mix them up.

Have your student choose a pair of matching mittens, flip them over to read the rhyming words, and then place the matching mittens on the kitten's paws.

Repeat until the kitten has tried on all the mittens.

New Teaching
(continued)

__Baby Bunnies__

Remove pages 241-244 from the activity book.

Cut the sheet with the mother rabbits in half horizontally. Cut out all the baby bunny cards on page 243. Your student may color the rabbits and bunnies, if desired.

Mix the baby bunny cards and place them in a pile on the table between the two mother rabbits.

Have your student select a card from the pile and read the word aloud. He should then determine whether the word belongs with the -ing rabbit or the -ang rabbit, and then place the baby rabbit card on the appropriate mother rabbit.

Continue until all the baby bunnies have found homes.

Practice Reading Words

Have your student practice reading the words on Word Cards 146-155.

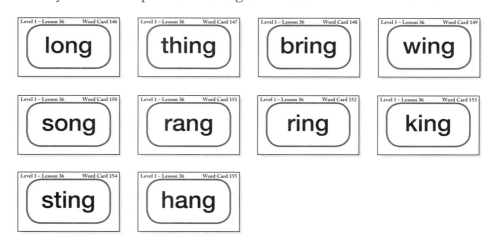

File the Word Cards behind the Review divider of the Reading Review Box.

New Teaching
(continued)

Practice Fluency

Remove pages 245-247 from the activity book.

Have your student read from the Practice Sheet.

Read-Aloud Time

Read a Story or Poem

Read aloud to your student for twenty minutes.

Track Your Progress

Mark the Progress Chart

Have your student mark Lesson 36 on the Progress Chart.

Lesson 36: Consonant Team NG

Lesson 37 - Read "The Bat and King Sam" and "The Long Nap"

In this lesson, students will read two short stories that give them practice with words containing <u>ng</u>, and discuss the five senses.

You will need: ☐ *Blast Off to Reading!* pages 249-252   ☐ a small snack

☐ *The Runt Pig* book   (apple, cracker, etc.)

Elijah 1/3/19

Before You Begin

Preview the Five Senses

Authors often use the five senses of taste, sight, sound, touch, and smell in their imagery and description. In today's activity, your student will practice distinguishing and discussing the five senses. You will need to provide a small snack for this activity.

Review

Review the Phonogram Cards that are behind the Review divider in your student's Reading Review Box. Show the card to your student and have him say the sound(s). If necessary, remind your student of the sound(s).

Review the Word Cards that are behind the Review divider in your student's Reading Review Box. If your student has difficulty reading the word, build the word with letter tiles and have your student sound it out using the procedure shown in Appendix C: Full Blending Procedure.

New Teaching

Complete Activity Sheet

"Today we will use our five senses to describe a food." Give your student a small snack to eat, like a slice of apple or a cracker.

<u>**That Makes Sense!**</u>
Remove page 249 from the *Blast Off* activity book.

Set the five senses pie chart in front of your student. Point to each section of the chart as you discuss the questions below, adjusting the wording according to the snack provided.

- Point to the hand (sense of touch). "How does the apple feel?" *Possible answers: smooth, damp.*
- Point to the eye (sense of sight). "How does the apple look?" *Possible answers: red, shiny.*
- Point to the ear (sense of sound). "How does the apple sound when you bite it?" *Possible answers: crunchy, crisp.*
- Point to the nose (sense of smell). "How does the apple smell?" *Possible answers: sweet, tart.*
- Point to the mouth (sense of taste). "How does the apple taste?" *Possible answers: juicy, sweet, sour.*

"Writers often use descriptive words to explain what things look, feel, smell, sound, and taste like."

Read the Warm-Up Sheet for "The Bat and King Sam"

Don't Forget
You will need the flip side of this Warm-Up Sheet for the next story, "The Long Nap." If you won't be completing that portion of the lesson today, return this Warm-Up Sheet to the activity book for safe keeping.

Remove page 251 from the activity book.

Have your student practice reading words and phrases that will be encountered in "The Bat and King Sam."

Lesson 37: Read "The Bat and King Sam" and "The Long Nap"

New Teaching
(continued)

Teach Vocabulary and Activate Prior Knowledge

Point out the illustration of a cliff on the Warm-Up Sheet. "A *cliff* is a steep rock face, especially at the edge of the sea."

Point out the illustration of an oil lamp on the Warm-Up Sheet. "This is an *oil lamp*. Oil lamps work by putting a type of oil in the base and then lighting a wick, as you do with a candle. These lamps were used before there was electricity and are still often used for camping."

"Do you like to sing songs? What song makes you feel happy and cheerful?" Discuss your student's favorite songs to sing.

"In this next story, a very special animal sings songs to cheer up a new friend. Let's see what happens."

Read "The Bat and King Sam"

"Turn to page 199 in your reader and read 'The Bat and King Sam' aloud." Discuss your student's ideas for the questions below as you come to them.

After page 200: "Why do you think the king's pets and animals ran off?"

After page 205: "The king is sad at the beginning of the story. How do you think he feels at the end of the story? Why?"

Discuss the Five Senses

After reading the story, take out the five senses pie chart. "Listen to the following sentences and point to the sense that is being used."

- A shadow moved in the tree. *Student points to sight.*
- The bat got a yummy snack. *Student points to taste.*
- King Sam held the flowers near his nose. *Student points to smell.*
- King Sam sobbed loudly. *Student points to sound.*
- The bat gave King Sam a big hug. *Student points to touch.*

Story 2: "The Long Nap"

Read the Warm-Up Sheet for "The Long Nap"

Remove page 252 from the activity book.

Have your student practice reading words and phrases that will be encountered in "The Long Nap."

Teach Vocabulary and Activate Prior Knowledge

Point out the illustration of a finch on the Warm-Up Sheet. "A *finch* is a colorful songbird."

Point out the illustration of a fox den on the Warm-Up Sheet. "A *den* is a wild animal's hidden home or lair. For example, foxes and bears live in dens. Dens keep animals warm and safe."

"Pretend you are a baby bear and you are very tired. What is your favorite place to take a nap?" Discuss your student's ideas.

"What would be a bad place to take a nap if you were a baby bear?"

"Let's see what happens when the bear cub in this story takes a nap."

Read "The Long Nap"

"Turn to page 209 in your reader and read 'The Long Nap' aloud." Discuss your student's ideas for the questions below as you come to them.

After reading: "How many and what kind of creatures pass by the bear while he is sleeping? Skim the story to find out."

"The bear is able to take a long nap, but what could have made his nap much shorter?" *Possible answers: The bird could have landed on his nose, the spider could have bit him, the moths could have tickled his ear, and so on.*

Read-Aloud Time   Read a Story or Poem

Read aloud to your student for twenty minutes.

Track Your Progress   Mark the Progress Chart

Have your student mark Lesson 37 on the Progress Chart.

YAWN!

I don't know about you, but a long nap sounds pretty good to me right now. Do you have any idea how much energy it takes to bury a bone on a planet with no gravity?

A LOT! Dig, dig, dig. Float, float, float. Catch, catch, catch. Dig, dig, dig. I'm too pooped to party!

So if you don't mind, I'm just going to curl up next to Lesson 38 while you learn about this NK business. I trust you to tell me all about it ... later ...
zzzzzzzzzzzzznk!

Lesson 37: Read "The Bat and King Sam" and "The Long Nap"

Lesson 38 - Consonant Team NK

This lesson will teach words containing the consonant team nk.

You will need: ☐ Phonogram Card 32   ☐ *Blast Off to Reading!* pages 253-259
                ☐ Letter tile nk   ☐ Word Cards 156-165

Elijah 1/4/19

Before You Begin

Preview Consonant Team NK

nk The consonant team nk says /ngk/ as in *think*. Listen for the /ngk/ sound in the following words.

trunk   bank   stink   thank   rink

Consonant team nk influences the vowels a and i just as ng does. The vowels don't say their pure short vowel sound. Instead, the sound falls between the short and long vowel sound, as in the words *rank* and *think*.

This concept is generally easy for students to grasp, since it is difficult to say the pure short vowel sound in these word parts. It is easier to say the word parts correctly.

It is interesting to note that nk never combines with e to form words. There is no word part *enk*.

Listen to the *Phonogram Sounds* app for a demonstration of the phonogram sounds.

Store the new tile under the following label:

Consonant Teams

nk

Review

Review the Phonogram Cards that are behind the Review divider in your student's Reading Review Box. Show the card to your student and have him say the sound. If necessary, remind your student of the sound.

Review the Word Cards that are behind the Review divider in your student's Reading Review Box. If your student has difficulty reading the word, build the word with letter tiles and have your student sound it out using the procedure shown in Appendix C: Full Blending Procedure.

New Teaching

Teach New Letter Sounds

Teach the Phonogram Card for the consonant team <u>nk</u>.

1. Hold up the Phonogram Card and demonstrate the sound.
2. Have your student repeat the sound.

Mix in several other Phonogram Cards for mixed review and practice until your student can say the sounds accurately. File the new Phonogram Card behind the Review divider in the Reading Review Box.

Set out the new letter tile. nk

Mix in several other letter tiles for mixed review and practice with the new tile until your student can say the sound accurately.

Blend Sounds with Letter Tiles

Arrange the letter tiles as follows.

Point to the *ank* word part. "Say this word part." *Ank.*

Move the <u>nk</u> down to form the *ink* word part. "Say this word part." *Ink.*

Lesson 38: Consonant Team NK

New Teaching
(continued)

Repeat with word parts *onk* and *unk*, and then do mixed review until your student can easily read all four of these word parts.

"Let's make some words with *ank*." One at a time, build the words *bank, sank,* and *thank* and read them with your student.

"Let's make some words with *ink*." One at a time, build the words *think, clink,* and *drink* and read them with your student.

"Let's make some words with *onk*." One at a time, build the words *honk* and *bonk* and read them with your student.

"Let's make some words with *unk*." One at a time, build the words *hunk, bunk,* and *sunk* and read them with your student.

Play "Change the Word"

Build the word *pink.* p i nk

"What is this word?" *Pink.*

"I'm going to change the first letter of this word."

"What does this new word say?" Encourage your student to sound out the new word. *Rink.*

Continue to change one letter at a time to form the following words. Each time, have your student sound out the new word.

rink → shrink → shrunk

sunk → junk → bunk → bank → thank → think → ink

New Teaching
(continued)

Complete Activity Sheet

<u>Word Flippers for NK</u>

Remove pages 253-255 from the *Blast Off* activity book.

Refer to Appendix E for assembly instructions.

Have your student turn the pages and read the words that are formed.

Practice Reading Words

Have your student practice reading the words on Word Cards 156-165.

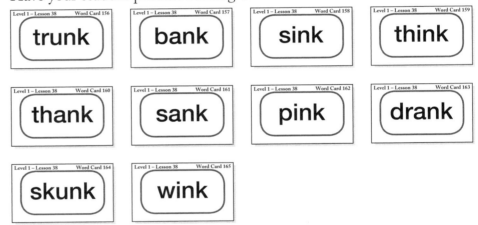

File the Word Cards behind the Review divider of the Reading Review Box.

Practice Fluency

Remove pages 257-259 from the activity book.

Have your student read from the Practice Sheet.

Lesson 38: Consonant Team NK

Read-Aloud Time   Read a Story or Poem

Read aloud to your student for twenty minutes.

Track Your Progress

Mark the Progress Chart

Have your student mark Lesson 38 on the Progress Chart.

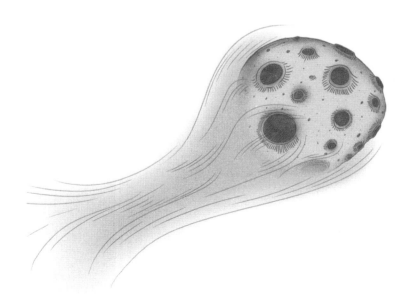

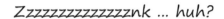

Zzzzzzzzzzzzznk ... huh?

Oh! I'm up! I'm up!
I'm ready to learn what you found out
about NK.

I thiNK you are so smart for doing that lesson all by
yourself. But thaNK you for rousing me from my
buNK so I can learn, too.

I hope I don't stiNK!
(wiNK wiNK)

Lesson 38: Consonant Team NK

Lesson 39 - Read "Frank Shrank" and "At Camp"

In this lesson, students will read two short stories that give them practice with words containing <u>nk</u>, and learn about cause and effect.

You will need: ☐ *Blast Off to Reading!* pages 261-264

☐ *The Runt Pig* book

Elijah 1/7/19

Review

Review the Phonogram Cards that are behind the Review divider in your student's Reading Review Box. Show the card to your student and have him say the sound(s). If necessary, remind your student of the sound(s).

Review the Word Cards that are behind the Review divider in your student's Reading Review Box. If your student has difficulty reading the word, build the word with letter tiles and have your student sound it out using the procedure shown in Appendix C: Full Blending Procedure.

New Teaching

Story 1: "Frank Shrank"

Complete Activity Sheet

"Anything that happens has a reason for happening. This is called *cause and effect*. Cause is *why* something happens; effect is *what* happens. This activity is all about cause and effect."

<u>Cause and Effect</u>
Remove pages 261-262 from the *Blast Off* activity book.

Cut out the cards in column 1 (cause) and column 2 (effect) on page 261.

Mix up the Cause cards and place them face up in a pile. Mix the Effect cards and spread them face up on the table. Have your student draw a Cause card, flip it over, read it aloud, and then choose the matching Effect card.

Continue until your student has matched all the cards.

New Teaching
(continued)

Don't Forget

You will need the flip side of this Warm-Up Sheet for the next story, "At Camp." If you won't be completing that portion of the lesson today, return this Warm-Up Sheet to the activity book for safe keeping.

Read the Warm-Up Sheet for "Frank Shrank"

Remove page 263 from the activity book.

Have your student practice reading words and phrases that will be encountered in "Frank Shrank."

Teach Vocabulary and Activate Prior Knowledge

Point out the illustration of an ink pad on the Warm-Up Sheet. "A *pad of ink* is like a little sponge filled with ink. You can press stamps into it to make words and designs, or you can press your fingers in it to make fingerprints."

Point out the illustration of a can of pop on the Warm-Up Sheet. "*Pop* is another word for soda. Depending on where you live, you might call it pop or soda. What is it called where you live?"

Point out the illustration of the ruler on the Warm-Up Sheet. "This is a *ruler*. Have you used a ruler to measure things?"

"Pretend that you are only two inches tall. Where would you sleep at night? How would you travel from place to place?" Ask your student how he might use various common objects, such as a teacup, a sponge, a ruler, and a straw.

"The boy in this story starts out big, but then gets very small. Let's see what kind of adventures he has."

Read "Frank Shrank"

"Turn to page 223 in your reader and read 'Frank Shrank' aloud." Discuss your student's ideas for the questions below as you come to them.

After page 226: "Do you think Frank is afraid of shrinking? Would you be? Why or why not?"

Lesson 39: Read "Frank Shrank" and "At Camp"

New Teaching
(continued)

After page 235: "What do you think will happen when Frank drinks that last drop of milk?"

After page 236: "Why is Frank happy to be big again?"

Discuss Cause and Effect in "Frank Shrank"

"There are several example of cause and effect in the story 'Frank Shrank.' Let's look at some of them."

"Turn to page 226. What causes Frank to shrink?" *Drinking the pink milk.*

"Turn to page 233. What causes Frank to fall?" *The wind of the fan.*

"Turn to page 234. Why does Frank end up in the pad of ink?" *Because he fell off the moth.*

Story 2: "At Camp"

Read the Warm-Up Sheet for "At Camp"

Remove page 264 from the activity book.

Have your student practice reading words and phrases that will be encountered in "At Camp."

Teach Vocabulary and Activate Prior Knowledge

Point out the illustration of a pack on the Warm-Up Sheet. "A *pack* is a small bag to carry items in. It is also called a *backpack, knapsack,* or *rucksack.*"

New Teaching
(continued)

"Have you ever been camping? What are some things you could do at a campsite?" *Possible answers: set up a tent, build a campfire, go fishing, collect leaves, watch the animals, roll out the sleeping bags.*

"The two boys in this story go camping on the top of a hill. Let's see what happens."

Read "At Camp"

"Turn to page 239 in your reader and read 'At Camp' aloud." Discuss your student's ideas for the questions below as you come to them.

After page 244: "Why do you think the fox is not in a rush?"

After page 250: "Look at the illustration. Why do you think the fox is staying near the tent?"

Read-Aloud Time

Read a Story or Poem

Read aloud to your student for twenty minutes.

Track Your Progress

Mark the Progress Chart

Have your student mark Lesson 39 on the Progress Chart.

Lesson 40 - Compound Words

This lesson will teach compound words, as well as the Leap Word <u>do</u>.

You will need: ☐ *Blast Off to Reading!* pages 265-275

☐ *Second set of letter tiles*

☐ *Word Cards 166-175*

Elijah 1/8/19

Before You Begin

Preview Compound Words

Compound words are special words that are made up of two smaller words, such as *sandbox*. Read the following examples and look for the two smaller words.

panfish   sunset   wetland   cannot   backpack

The small words that comprise the larger compound word have already been taught, so the compound words are 100% decodable.

In Level 2, students will learn a syllable division rule specifically for compound words.

Add Letter Tiles to the Magnetic White Board

Building compound words will require more letters. Add the remaining tiles from the second set of <u>a</u>-<u>z</u> letter tiles to complete your setup.

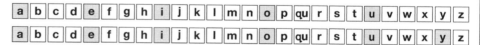

You may notice that there is a third <u>s</u> tile. Save it for Lesson 42.

Review

Review the Phonogram Cards that are behind the Review divider in your student's Reading Review Box. Show the card to your student and have him say the sound. If necessary, remind your student of the sound.

Review the Word Cards that are behind the Review divider in your student's Reading Review Box. If your student has difficulty reading the word, build the word with letter tiles and have your student sound it out using the procedure shown in Appendix C: Full Blending Procedure.

New Teaching

Teach Compound Words

Build the word *bathtub* with letter tiles. | b | a | th | t | u | b |

"The word *bathtub* has two smaller words in it. Can you find the two smaller words?" *Bath, tub.*

"Good! Two smaller words put together form a special type of word. We call this type of word a *compound word*."

Complete Activity Sheets

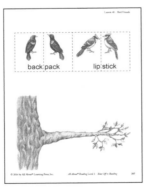

Bird Friends

Remove pages 265-267 from the *Blast Off* activity book.

Cut out the branch and the bird cards. Lay the birds on the table and mix them up. Your student should select two matching birds, set them on the branch side by side, and read the resulting compound word.

If you wish to identify the birds with your student, here is the list of species represented.

Card / Bird Species	Card / Bird Species
quicksand / cardinal	pigpen / scarlet tanager
bobcat / goldfinch	milkman / hairy woodpecker
bathtub / robin	catfish / rose-breasted grosbeak
itself / magpie	backpack / red-winged blackbird
cannot / meadowlark	lipstick / blue jay

New Teaching
(continued)

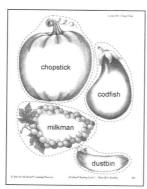

Chop-Chop
Remove pages 269-271 from the activity book.

Cut out the knife and the foods.

Have your student pretend to cut each compound word between its two smaller words. He should then read each smaller word, and then the entire compound word.

Practice Reading Words

Have your student practice reading the words on Word Cards 166-174.

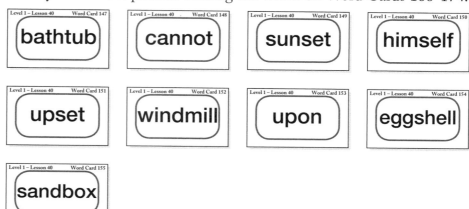

File the Word Cards behind the Review divider of the Reading Review Box.

Teach a Leap Word: *do*

Show Word Card 175 to your student.

We are treating the word *do* as a Leap Word because it contains the third sound of <u>o</u>, which has not been taught yet.

"This word is *do*, as in *What did you do today?*"

Point to the <u>o</u>. "The <u>o</u> doesn't say the sound we expect it to."

Review this Leap Word several times today and then file it behind the Review divider in the Reading Review Box.

New Teaching
(continued)

Practice Fluency

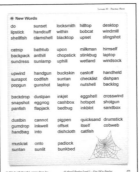

Remove pages 273-275 from the activity book.

Have your student read from the Practice Sheet.

Read-Aloud Time

Read a Story or Poem

Read aloud to your student for twenty minutes.

Track Your Progress

Mark the Progress Chart

Have your student mark Lesson 40 on the Progress Chart.

Lesson 40: Compound Words

Lesson 41 - Read "Cobweb the Cat" and "Yuck!"

In this lesson, students will read two short stories that give them practice with compound words, and discuss realism vs. fantasy.

You will need: ☐ *Blast Off to Reading!* pages 277-283

☐ *Cobweb the Cat* book   ☐ Optional: map or globe

Elijah 1/9/19

Before You Begin

Today your student will read the first two stories in the third reader, *Cobweb the Cat*.

The subtle underlining that is found in the first two readers is no longer used in this reader because most students don't need it. If your student would still benefit from the underlining, feel free to pencil it in or continue to use the top edge of the Viewfinder Bookmark.

Many of the stories in this third collection are longer. Remember that you can stop the lesson after 20 minutes (or whatever time you have determined to be the ideal lesson length) and continue the story during your next class. Completing an entire lesson in one session is not expected.

Words and concepts introduced in earlier lessons continue to be reviewed in these stories.

Review

Review the Phonogram Cards that are behind the Review divider in your student's Reading Review Box. Show the card to your student and have him say the sound(s). If necessary, remind your student of the sound(s).

Review the Word Cards that are behind the Review divider in your student's Reading Review Box. If your student has difficulty reading the word, build the word with letter tiles and have your student sound it out using the procedure shown in Appendix C: Full Blending Procedure.

New Teaching

Story 1: "Cobweb the Cat"

Read the Warm-Up Sheet for "Cobweb the Cat"

Remove page 277 from the *Blast Off* activity book.

Have your student practice reading words and phrases that will be encountered in "Cobweb the Cat."

Teach Vocabulary and Activate Prior Knowledge

Point out the illustration of a feather duster on the Warm-Up Sheet. "This is a *feather duster*. People use feather dusters to dust the furniture in their houses."

Point out the illustration of a windmill on the Warm-Up Sheet. "A *windmill* is a building with big sails on it that spin like a fan in the wind."

Find the Netherlands on a map or globe. "The next story is set in the Netherlands, a country in Western Europe on the North Sea. The Netherlands is famous for its many windmills, which were once used to pump water and to help make products like paper, mustard, chalk, paint, and grain."

"The cat in this story lives in a windmill. Let's see what he does all day."

Read "Cobweb the Cat"

"Turn to page 9 in your reader and read 'Cobweb the Cat' aloud." Discuss your student's ideas for the questions below as you come to them.

After page 19: "What do you think Cobweb is hunting?"

New Teaching
(continued)

After reading: Point out pages 13-15. "Is Cobweb actually checking the milk, fixing the tub, and dusting the desktop? What is he doing instead?"

Discuss Realism vs. Fantasy

"Do you think the cat in this story really could have done all the things he did? Why or why not?"

"Go back to the beginning of the story and look for sentences that describe something that the cat couldn't do in real life." *Possible answers: check the milk, fix the bathtub, dust the desktop, feed the fish, hang his rug, sing a song.*

"Why do you think a cat couldn't do those things?"

"This story is fantasy. That means that it isn't real—it is make-believe."

"I will read a list of activities, and you will tell me if the activity could happen in real life or if it is fantasy." For each fantasy activity, ask your student why it couldn't happen.

"A friend saved up his money to buy a new toy." *It could happen.*
"A donkey invited us to a barbecue." *It's fantasy.*
"The daisies sang me a song about rain." *It's fantasy.*
"My sister did somersaults on the playground." *It could happen.*

Complete Activity Sheet

"In this activity, you'll decide which things a real cat can do."

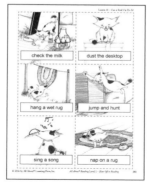

<u>Can a Real Cat Do It?</u>
Remove pages 279-281 from the activity book.

Cut out the cards on page 279.

Have your student look at the illustrations and read the text. If the action is something that a real cat could do, have your student place the card on the large illustration of the real cat.

If your student places a "fantasy" action on the real cat, allow him to defend his choice. Ask your student to explain his answer, and then accept it at this early stage.

Story 2: "Yuck!"

Read the Warm-Up Sheet for "Yuck!"

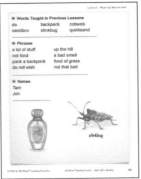

Remove page 283 from the activity book.

Have your student practice reading words and phrases that will be encountered in "Yuck!"

Point out the name *Tam* in the Names section. "Tam is a nickname for Tamara."

Teach Vocabulary and Activate Prior Knowledge

Point out the illustration of a stinkbug on the Warm-Up Sheet. "A *stinkbug* is a small bug that lets off a bad smell. Stinkbugs might stick to your clothes, so be careful!"

Point out the illustration of perfume on the Warm-Up Sheet. "This is *perfume*. Perfume comes in many different scents. People wear perfume so that they smell good. Do you know anyone who wears perfume?"

"What are some things or activities that you don't like? Why don't you like them?"

"How could a friend convince you to try something you don't like?"

"The girl in this story doesn't like a lot of things—at first. Let's see if she ends up liking anything at all."

Read "Yuck!"

"Turn to page 25 in your reader and read 'Yuck!' aloud." Discuss your student's ideas for the questions below as you come to them.

After page 32: "Why isn't Tam fond of the hill?"

After page 35: "So far Tam has ended up liking all the things she disliked at first. Do you think she will end up liking the stinkbug? Why?"

New Teaching
(continued)

After page 38: "Why do you think Jon is hiding the stinkbug? What might he do with it?"

After reading: "Why do you think Tam is so quick to dislike things, even before she knows what they are?"

"Do you think this story could be mostly real, or is it fantasy? Why?"

Read-Aloud Time

Read a Story or Poem

Read aloud to your student for twenty minutes.

Track Your Progress

Mark the Progress Chart

Have your student mark Lesson 41 on the Progress Chart.

Again with the CATS!

OK, you did a galactically fabulous job of reading these stories, but can't you do your old friend Rocket a tiny little favor?

You see, I'm spinning out of my orbit with all these clawed creatures, so if you don't mind ...

... enough with the CATS!

More stinkbugs, fewer CATS!

250

Lesson 42 - Plural Words

This lesson will teach plural words and verbs ending in <u>s</u> and <u>es</u>.

You will need: ☐ *Blast Off to Reading!* pages 285-289

☐ Extra <u>s</u> letter tile

☐ Word Cards 176-185

Before You Begin

Preview Plural Words

The <u>s</u> at the end of a plural word can say either /s/ or /z/. Most students will naturally say the correct sound for the letter <u>s</u>, since it is actually hard to say the wrong sound. But if your student has difficulty, remind him to say the singular form of the word first, and then the plural form. He will naturally pronounce the word correctly.

Read the following examples of plural words and listen for the /s/ or /z/ sound.

/s/:	lips	sinks	hilltops	belts	rats
/z/:	flags	spills	stems	fishes	boxes

It is interesting to note that the letter <u>s</u> says /z/ after vowel sounds (as in *plays*) and after voiced consonants (as in *bugs*).

The suffix <u>es</u> is found after the sounds /s/, /z/, /ch/, /sh/, and /ks/. The syllable <u>es</u> at the end of a word is unaccented, and therefore the vowel sound is muffled. In normal speech, <u>es</u> often sounds like /ĭz/ instead of /ĕz/.

Add a Letter Tile to the Magnetic White Board

In today's lesson, your student will begin building plural words. Add the third <u>s</u> tile to your letter tile setup.

Preview Verbs Ending in S and ES

Many present tense verbs end in <u>s</u> or <u>es</u>, such as *checks*, *mixes*, and *hits*. Students will encounter these words on the Practice Sheets and in the upcoming short stories. Because of their experience with plural words, it will be easy for them to decode these verbs.

Review

Review the Phonogram Cards that are behind the Review divider in your student's Reading Review Box. Show the card to your student and have him say the sound. If necessary, remind your student of the sound.

Review the Word Cards that are behind the Review divider in your student's Reading Review Box. If your student has difficulty reading the word, build the word with letter tiles and have your student sound it out using the procedure shown in Appendix C: Full Blending Procedure.

New Teaching

Teach Plural Words

Build the word *hats* with letter tiles.　| h | a | t | s |

Cover the s with your finger.

"We say one *hat*..."　

"...and we say two *hats*."　| h | a | t | s |

"*Hats* is **plural** because it means **more than one**."

"I'll say a word and you make it plural."

"One *map*, two _____." If necessary, prompt your student to say *maps*.

"One *ant*, two _____." *Ants.*

"One *star*, two _____." *Stars.*

"At the end of a word, the s can say either /s/ or /z/. First try the /s/ sound, and if that doesn't sound right, try the /z/ sound."

Build the following words and have your student read them.

| c | u | p | s |　　| b | u | g | s |　　| t | e | n | t | s |

Build the word *glasses* with tiles.　| g | l | a | s | s | e | s |

Cover the e-s with your finger.

"We say one *glass*..."　

New Teaching
(continued)

"...and we say two *glasses*."

"*Glasses* is **plural** because it means **more than one**."

Build the following words and have your student read them.

Complete Activity Sheet

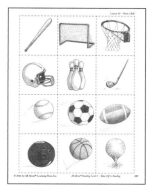

Have a Ball

Remove pages 285-286 from the *Blast Off* activity book.

Cut out the twelve sports items. Place the six balls in one group with the words facing down. Mix them up.

Place the six items of sports equipment in another group with the words facing down.

Have your student match each ball with the corresponding piece of sports equipment. He should then flip them over and read the singular and plural versions of the words.

Practice Reading Words

Have your student practice reading the words on Word Cards 176-185.

File the Word Cards behind the Review divider of the Reading Review Box.

New Teaching
(continued)

Practice Fluency

Remove pages 287-289 from the activity book.

Have your student read from the Practice Sheet.

Read-Aloud Time

Read a Story or Poem

Read aloud to your student for twenty minutes.

Track Your Progress

Mark the Progress Chart

Have your student mark Lesson 42 on the Progress Chart.

Lesson 42: Plural Words

Lesson 43 - Read "Ten Wishes" and "Fast Fun"

In this lesson, students will read two short stories that give them practice with plural words, and complete an activity about rhyme.

You will need: ☐ Blast Off to Reading! pages 291-295

☐ Cobweb the Cat book

Review

Review the Phonogram Cards that are behind the Review divider in your student's Reading Review Box. Show the card to your student and have him say the sound(s). If necessary, remind your student of the sound(s).

Review the Word Cards that are behind the Review divider in your student's Reading Review Box. If your student has difficulty reading the word, build the word with letter tiles and have your student sound it out using the procedure shown in Appendix C: Full Blending Procedure.

New Teaching

Story 1: "Ten Wishes"

Read the Warm-Up Sheet for "Ten Wishes"

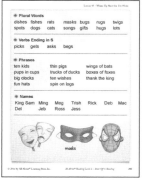

Remove page 291 from the activity book.

Have your student practice reading words and phrases that will be encountered in "Ten Wishes."

Teach Vocabulary and Activate Prior Knowledge

Point out the illustrations of the masks on the Warm-Up Sheet. "A *mask* is a disguise that covers all or part of your face. Do you recognize any of these masks?"

"Have you ever dressed up in a costume with a mask? What kind of mask was it?"

"Suppose that for one day you could have the one thing you want most in the world. What would you ask for?" Discuss your student's ideas.

"Let's see what the children in this story would ask for."

Read "Ten Wishes"

"Turn to page 41 in your reader and read 'Ten Wishes' aloud." Discuss your student's ideas for the question below when you come to it.

After reading: "Which of these wishes would you like the most? The least? Why?"

Your student may notice that the king in "Ten Wishes" is the same King Sam as in the story "The Bat and King Sam."

Complete Activity Sheet

"Did you notice that many of the wishes rhyme? In this activity, you'll match the characters with their rhyming wishes."

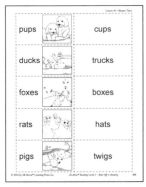

Rhyme Time
Remove page 293 from the activity book.

Cut out the character cards and rhyme cards.

Mix the character cards and place them face down in a pile. Mix the rhyme cards and spread them face up on the table. Have your student draw the character cards one at a time, read the card out loud, and then choose the matching rhyme card.

Continue until your student has matched all the cards.

New Teaching
(continued)

Read the Warm-Up Sheet for "Fast Fun"

Remove page 295 from the activity book.

Have your student practice reading words and phrases that will be encountered in "Fast Fun."

Teach Vocabulary and Activate Prior Knowledge

Point out the illustration of a dishcloth on the Warm-Up Sheet. "A *dishcloth* is a piece of fabric used to wash or dry dishes. It's also called a *dishrag*, *washcloth*, and *kitchen cloth*. What does your family call it?"

Point out the illustration of children playing leapfrog on the Warm-Up Sheet. "These kids are playing a game called *leapfrog*. In this game, one person bends down and another person vaults right over his back, like a frog."

"Do you know what a tongue twister is? It's a silly sentence that's hard to say, like *Rubber baby buggy bumpers*. Do you know any tongue twisters?"

"Let's see if you can say the tongue twisters in the next story."

Read "Fast Fun"

"Turn to page 57 in your reader and read 'Fast Fun' aloud."

Encourage your student to repeat each tongue twister several times in a row. How fast can he go?

Read-Aloud Time   Read a Story or Poem

Read aloud to your student for twenty minutes.

Track Your
Progress

Mark the Progress Chart

Have your student mark Lesson 43 on the Progress Chart.

Lesson 43: Read "Ten Wishes" and "Fast Fun"

Lesson 44 - Additional Sounds for A, I, and C

This lesson will teach additional sounds for the letters <u>a</u>, <u>i</u>, and <u>c</u>.

You will need: ☐ Phonogram Cards 4, 11, and 16

☐ Letter tiles <u>a</u>, <u>i</u>, and <u>c</u>

☐ *Blast Off to Reading!* page 297

Before You Begin

Look Back at Previous Progress

Your student has come a long way! He can now decode any CVC (consonant-vowel-consonant) word, as well as words containing these concepts:

- words with blends
- words with consonant teams <u>th</u>, <u>sh</u>, <u>ch</u>, <u>ck</u>, <u>ng</u>, and <u>nk</u>
- compound words

The one thing that ties these words together is that they are all short vowel words with closed syllables.

The sequence has been very intentional. We wanted your student to become confident in reading short vowel words because it is a developmentally appropriate approach to teaching reading.

And starting with this lesson, we're ready to build on this solid base!

Look Ahead to Remaining Lessons

As you know by now, the vowels and some of the consonants have more than one sound. Your student has learned the first, most common, sound for these letters, and now it is time to learn the remaining sounds.

Here's a summary of the remaining lessons in Level 1:

- The "new concept" lessons (Lessons 44, 46, 48, and 50) teach the remaining sounds of the letters. There are no new Word Cards taught during these lessons; the teaching time is devoted to the new phonogram sounds.

- The "read a story" lessons (Lessons 45, 47, 49, and 51) present eight new stories. These stories provide great practice with the words taught in Lessons 1–42 and help your student build fluency and reading stamina. No new words are introduced.

- Lesson 52 puts all the newly learned long vowel sounds to use, and seven open syllable words are taught, including *she*, *go*, and *we*.

- The final lesson, Lesson 53, includes two stories that give practice with these new open syllable words.

Preview the Sounds of the Letters

In this lesson, your student will be learning the remaining sounds of a̲, i̲, and c̲. As a quick reminder, the letter a̲ can say three sounds:

- /ă/ as in *apple*, known as the short sound (taught in Lesson 1)
- /ā/ as in *acorn*, known as the long sound
- /ah/ as in *father*

The letter i̲ can say three sounds:

- /ĭ/ as in *itchy*, known as the short sound (taught in Lesson 8)
- /ī/ as in *ivy*, known as the long sound
- /ē/ as in *radio*

The letter c̲ can say two sounds:

- /k/ as in *cat*, or hard c̲ (taught in Lesson 4)
- /s/ as in *city*, or soft c̲

 Listen to the *Phonogram Sounds* app for a demonstration of the phonogram sounds.

 If you are using *Reading Games with Ziggy the Zebra*, you can practice these phonograms by playing "Ziggy Plays with Penguins."

Review

Review the Phonogram Cards that are behind the Review divider in your student's Reading Review Box. Show the card to your student and have him say the sound. If necessary, remind your student of the sound.

Review the Word Cards that are behind the Review divider in your student's Reading Review Box. If your student has difficulty reading the word, build the word with letter tiles and have your student sound it out using the procedure shown in Appendix C: Full Blending Procedure.

New Teaching

In future lessons, your student will learn when each of these letters can say their first, second, and third sounds.

Teach New Letter Sounds

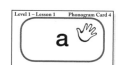

Take out Phonogram Card 4 and show it to your student.

"You already know that the letter a says /ă/. But it also makes two other sounds: /ā/ and /ah/. So the letter a makes three sounds: /ă/, /ā/, and /ah/. Repeat after me: /ă/–/ā/–/ah/." *Student repeats.*

Take out Phonogram Card 16 and show it to your student.

"You already know that the letter i says /ĭ/. But it also makes two other sounds: /ī/ and /ē/. So the letter i makes three sounds: /ĭ/, /ī/, and /ē/. Repeat after me: /ĭ/–/ī/–/ē/." *Student repeats.*

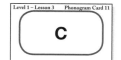

Take out Phonogram Card 11 and show it to your student.

"You already know that the letter c says /k/. But it also makes another sound, /s/. So the letter c makes two sounds: /k/ and /s/. Repeat after me: /k/–/s/." *Student repeats.*

Set out the letter tiles and practice until your student can say the sounds accurately.

New Teaching
(continued)

Complete Activity Sheet

Load the Train

Remove page 297 from the *Blast Off* activity book.

Give your student something fun to use for markers, like raisins, M&Ms, coins, jelly beans, or Cheerios.

Randomly call out the sounds of the letters. For instance, for the letter i, ask your student to place a jelly bean over the letter that can say /ĭ/–/ī/–/ē/.

As you call each sound or group of sounds, your student should put a marker over the corresponding letter. When your student has filled all eight parts of the train, he says "Choo-choo!"

Read-Aloud Time

Read a Story or Poem

Read aloud to your student for twenty minutes.

Track Your Progress

Mark the Progress Chart

Have your student mark Lesson 44 on the Progress Chart.

Lesson 44: Additional Sounds for A, I, and C

Lesson 45 - Read "The Lost List" and "No Mud for Max"

In this lesson, students will read two short stories and skim the text to answer questions.

You will need: ☐ Blast Off to Reading! pages 299-303

☐ Cobweb the Cat book

☐ Optional: M&Ms, raisins, or nuts

Review

Review the Phonogram Cards that are behind the Review divider in your student's Reading Review Box. Show the card to your student and have him say the sound(s). If necessary, remind your student of the sound(s).

Review the Word Cards that are behind the Review divider in your student's Reading Review Box. If your student has difficulty reading the word, build the word with letter tiles and have your student sound it out using the procedure shown in Appendix C: Full Blending Procedure.

New Teaching

Story 1: "The Lost List"

Read the Warm-Up Sheet for "The Lost List"

Remove page 299 from the activity book.

Have your student practice reading words and phrases that will be encountered in "The Lost List."

Teach Vocabulary and Activate Prior Knowledge

Point out the illustration of hot cross buns on the Warm-Up Sheet. "A *hot cross bun* is a spiced, sweet bun made with currants or raisins and marked with a cross on the top."

Point out the illustration of a badger on the Warm-Up Sheet. "This is a *badger*. Badgers are strong, nocturnal mammals in the weasel family. They usually have a gray and black coat."

"There is a badger in the next story that likes to help with the grocery shopping. Let's see if he does a good job."

Read "The Lost List"

"Turn to page 69 in your reader and read 'The Lost List' aloud." Discuss your student's ideas for the questions below as you come to them.

After page 73: "Uh-oh, Finn lost the list! Do you remember the four items he is supposed to get?"

After page 78: "Did Finn get all the right items? How do you think his mother will react to his purchases?"

After reading: "Why do you think Mom and Dad aren't mad at Finn?"

Complete Activity Sheet

"Now let's see if you can remember the facts in the story."

Check the Facts
Remove page 301 from the *Blast Off* activity book.

Have your student read each question in the first column and then mark his answer in the appropriate *yes* or *no* column. If desired, mark each answer with an M&M, raisin, or nut.

New Teaching
(continued)

Read the Warm-Up Sheet for "No Mud for Max"

Remove page 303 from the activity book.

Have your student practice reading words and phrases that will be encountered in "No Mud for Max."

Teach Vocabulary and Activate Prior Knowledge

Point out the illustration of the hippopotamus on the Warm-Up Sheet. "This is a *hippopotamus*, or *hippo* for short. A hippo is a large African mammal with thick skin, huge jaws, and big tusks. Hippos live on land and in the water."

Point out the illustration of a remote control on the Warm-Up Sheet. "This is a *remote control*. You probably have a remote control for your television. Remote controls are used to operate machines or even toys from a distance."

"Have you ever lost a toy in a tree or in a hole or under something? How did you get it back?"

"The hippo in this story loses his favorite toy. Let's see if he gets it back."

Read "No Mud for Max"

"Turn to page 83 in your reader and read 'No Mud for Max' aloud." Discuss your student's ideas for the questions below as you come to them.

After page 87: "If you were to help Max, how would you get the plane out of the mud?"

After page 91: "What do you think is going to happen?"

New Teaching
(continued)

After reading: "Do you think Max has anything in common with Tam from the story 'Yuck!'?" *Possible answer: They both think they don't like something but then find out it is not so bad.*

Read-Aloud Time

Read a Story or Poem

Read aloud to your student for twenty minutes.

Track Your Progress

Mark the Progress Chart

Have your student mark Lesson 45 on the Progress Chart.

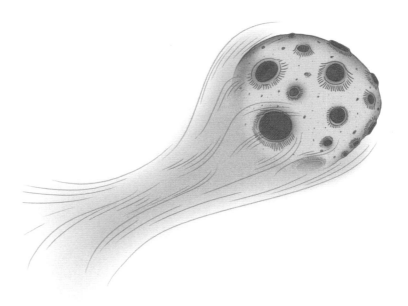

Lesson 45: Read "The Lost List" and "No Mud for Max"

Lesson 46 - Additional Sounds for O and G

This lesson will teach additional sounds for the letters o and g.

You will need: ☐ Phonogram Cards 9 and 20

☐ Letter tiles o and g

☐ Blast Off to Reading! page 305

Before You Begin

Preview the Sounds of the Letters

In this lesson, your student will be learning the remaining three sounds of o and the remaining sound of g. As a quick reminder, the letter o can say four sounds:

- /ŏ/ as in *otter*, known as the short sound (taught in Lesson 10)
- /ō/ as in *open*, known as the long sound
- /ōō/ as in *to*
- /ŭ/ as in *oven*

And the letter g can say two sounds:

- /g/ as in *goat*, or hard g (taught in Lesson 4)
- /j/ as in *gem*, or soft g

 Listen to the *Phonogram Sounds* app for a demonstration of the phonogram sounds.

 If you are using *Reading Games with Ziggy the Zebra*, you can practice these phonograms by playing "Ziggy Plays with Penguins."

Review

Review the Phonogram Cards that are behind the Review divider in your student's Reading Review Box. Show the card to your student and have him say the sound. If necessary, remind your student of the sound.

Review
(continued)

Word Cards

Review the Word Cards that are behind the Review divider in your student's Reading Review Box. If your student has difficulty reading the word, build the word with letter tiles and have your student sound it out using the procedure shown in Appendix C: Full Blending Procedure.

New Teaching

Teach New Letter Sounds

Take out Phonogram Card 20 and show it to your student.

"You already know that the letter o says /ŏ/. But it also makes three other sounds: /ō/, /ōō/, and /ŭ/. So the letter o makes four sounds: /ŏ/, /ō/, /ōō/, and /ŭ/. Repeat after me: /ŏ/–/ō/–/ōō/–/ŭ/." *Student repeats.*

Take out Phonogram Card 9 and show it to your student.

"You already know that the letter g says /g/. But it also makes another sound, /j/. So the letter g makes two sounds: /g/ and /j/. Repeat after me: /g/–/j/." *Student repeats.*

Set out the letter tiles and practice until your student can say the sounds accurately.

o g

Complete Activity Sheet

<u>Ride 'em, Cowboy!</u>
Remove page 305 from the *Blast Off* activity book.

Give your student something fun to use for markers, like raisins, M&Ms, coins, jelly beans, or Cheerios.

Randomly call out the sounds of the letters. For instance, for the letter g, ask your student to place a jelly bean over the letter that can say /g/ –/j/. As you call each sound or group of sounds, your student should put a marker over the corresponding letter. When your student has filled all six saddles, he says "Ride 'em, Cowboy!"

Lesson 46: Additional Sounds for O and G

Read-Aloud Time Read a Story or Poem

Read aloud to your student for twenty minutes.

Track Your Progress

Mark the Progress Chart

Have your student mark Lesson 46 on the Progress Chart.

It's been a while, hasn't it?

I've been floating around the universe mulling over these compound and plural words. Aren't they astounding? So now I don't need to fly just <u>one</u> rocket, because I can fly <u>two</u> rockets!

And I had another great idea to change my name to a compound word. I am no longer Rocket the Dog, but ...
ROCKET THE SPACEDOG
Master of the Universe

Pretty stylish, eh? I'm going to have it printed in stardust on my air bubble.
Your turn—what's your new compound space name?

Lesson 46: Additional Sounds for O and G

Lesson 47 - Read "Pip the Milkman" and "The Duck Egg"

In this lesson, students will read two short stories and learn about character motivation.

You will need: ☐ Blast Off to Reading! pages 307-310

☐ Cobweb the Cat book

Review

Review the Phonogram Cards that are behind the Review divider in your student's Reading Review Box. Show the card to your student and have him say the sound(s). If necessary, remind your student of the sound(s).

Review the Word Cards that are behind the Review divider in your student's Reading Review Box. If your student has difficulty reading the word, build the word with letter tiles and have your student sound it out using the procedure shown in Appendix C: Full Blending Procedure.

New Teaching

Story 1: "Pip the Milkman"

Complete Activity Sheet

> This activity explains why Gil is so upset when the milk isn't delivered in the upcoming story. It gives insight into the character's motivation.

> You may need to explain to your student that pancakes are made with flour, eggs, and milk.

"If you've ever helped make a meal or dessert at home, you know that you need specific ingredients to cook with. In this activity, you'll help the chef find the ingredients he needs."

Where's the Milk?
Remove page 307 from the *Blast Off* activity book.

Cut out the nine food cards and place them face up in a pile.

Point to the illustration of the chef. "This is Gil, which is a nickname for Gilbert. Gil is a chef who runs a special kind of restaurant called a pancake house. He needs specific ingredients in order to make his breakfast foods."

New Teaching
(continued)

Have your student choose one food card at a time. If the food is one that would be used in Gil's restaurant, the student should place the food next to Gil. If the food would not be used to make breakfast food, the student may simply say "No!" and place the card in a pile to one side.

"If you were Gil, how would you feel if the delivery truck brought you hot dogs instead of milk? What would you do?"

Read the Warm-Up Sheet for "Pip the Milkman"

Remove page 309 from the activity book.

Have your student practice reading words and phrases that will be encountered in "Pip the Milkman."

 Don't Forget You will need the flip side of this Warm-Up Sheet for the next story, "The Duck Egg." If you won't be completing that portion of the lesson today, return this Warm-Up Sheet to the activity book for safekeeping.

Teach Vocabulary and Activate Prior Knowledge

Point out the illustration of a horse-drawn wagon on the Warm-Up Sheet. "This is a *horse-drawn wagon*. Wagons like this were used a long time ago to deliver goods like milk and ice."

"If you could open a restaurant or shop, what kind would it be? Why?"

"Let's see what happens to the owner of the restaurant in this story."

Read "Pip the Milkman"

"Turn to page 95 in your reader and read 'Pip the Milkman' aloud." Discuss your student's ideas for the questions below as you come to them.

After page 102: "Why is it so important for Gil to have milk?"

After page 104: "Why is Gil angry at the cat? Why does the cat nip at him?"

After page 106: "Now Gil is grinning. Why do you think his mood changes from angry to happy?"

Lesson 47: Read "Pip the Milkman" and "The Duck Egg"

New Teaching
(continued)

Read the Warm-Up Sheet for "The Duck Egg"

Remove page 310 from the activity book.

Have your student practice reading words and phrases that will be encountered in "The Duck Egg."

Teach Vocabulary and Activate Prior Knowledge

Point out the illustration of a duck on the Warm-Up Sheet. "The setting for the next story is a lake, and the main character is a duck."

Point out the illustration of a muskrat on the Warm-Up Sheet. "Another animal in this story is a *muskrat*. A muskrat is a large rodent that lives in the water. Muskrats have thick, light-brown fur and a strong odor."

Point out the illustration of a hornet on the Warm-Up Sheet. "This is a *hornet*. A hornet is similar to a wasp. Why do you think some people call hornets *pests*?"

"Have you ever seen a nest with eggs in it? What kind of dangers do unprotected eggs face?" *Possible answers: The nest or eggs could fall out and break, another animal could steal the eggs.*

"Let's see what happens to the duck egg in this story."

Read "The Duck Egg"

"Turn to page 109 in your reader and read 'The Duck Egg' aloud." Discuss your student's ideas for the question below when you come to it.

After page 111: "Where do you think the mother duck is? Why would she leave the egg unprotected?"

Read-Aloud Time   Read a Story or Poem

Read aloud to your student for twenty minutes.

Track Your Progress

Mark the Progress Chart

Have your student mark Lesson 47 on the Progress Chart.

Lesson 48 - Additional Sounds for E, U, Y, and CH

This lesson will teach additional sounds for the letters e, u, y, and consonant team ch.

You will need: ☐ Phonogram Cards 12, 23, 24, and 29

☐ Letter tiles e, u, red y, and ch

☐ Blast Off to Reading! page 311

Before You Begin

Preview the Sounds of the Letters

In this lesson, your student will be learning the remaining sounds of e, u, y, and ch. As a quick reminder, the letter e can say two sounds:

- /ĕ/ as in *echo*, known as the short sound (taught in Lesson 14)
- /ē/ as in *even*, known as the long sound

The letter u can say three sounds:

- /ŭ/ as in *udder*, known as the short sound (taught in Lesson 12)
- /ū/ as in *unit*, known as the long sound
- /o͝o/ as in *put*

The letter y can say four sounds:

- /y/ as in *yarn*, a consonant sound (taught in Lesson 4)
- /ĭ/ as in *gym*, a vowel sound
- /ī/ as in *my*, a vowel sound
- /ē/ as in *happy*, a vowel sound

And consonant team ch can say three sounds:

- /ch/ as in *child* (taught in Lesson 22)
- /k/ as in *school*
- /sh/ as in *chef*

 Listen to the *Phonogram Sounds* app for a demonstration of the phonogram sounds.

| **Before You Begin** (continued) | | If you are using *Reading Games with Ziggy the Zebra*, you can practice these phonograms by playing "Ziggy Plays with Penguins." |

Review

Review the Phonogram Cards that are behind the Review divider in your student's Reading Review Box. Show the card to your student and have him say the sound. If necessary, remind your student of the sound.

Review the Word Cards that are behind the Review divider in your student's Reading Review Box. If your student has difficulty reading the word, build the word with letter tiles and have your student sound it out using the procedure shown in Appendix C: Full Blending Procedure.

Shuffle the cards behind the **Mastered** dividers and choose a selection for review.

New Teaching

Teach New Letter Sounds

Take out Phonogram Card 24 and show it to your student.

"You already know that the letter e says /ĕ/. But it also makes another sound: /ē/. So the letter e makes two sounds: /ĕ/ and /ē/. Repeat after me: /ĕ/–/ē/." *Student repeats.*

Take out Phonogram Card 23 and show it to your student.

"You already know that the letter u says /ŭ/. But it also makes two other sounds: /ū/ and /o͞o/. So the letter u makes three sounds: /ŭ/, /ū/, and /o͞o/. Repeat after me: /ŭ/–/ū/–/o͞o/." *Student repeats.*

New Teaching
(continued)

Take out Phonogram Card 12 and show it to your student.

"You already know that the letter y̱ says /y/. But it also makes three other sounds: / ĭ /, /ī/, and /ē/. So the letter y̱ makes four sounds: /y/, /ĭ/, /ī/, and /ē/. Repeat after me: /y/–/ĭ/–/ī/–/ē/." *Student repeats.*

Take out Phonogram Card 29 and show it to your student.

"You already know that consonant team c̱ẖ says /ch/. But it also makes two other sounds: /k/ and /sh/. So consonant team c̱ẖ makes three sounds: /ch/, /k/, and /sh/. Repeat after me: /ch/–/k/–/sh/." *Student repeats.*

Set out the letter tiles and practice until your student can say the sounds accurately.

`e` `u` `red` `y` `ch`

Complete Activity Sheet

Dump Trucks
Remove page 311 from the *Blast Off* activity book.

Give your student something fun to use for markers, like raisins, M&Ms, coins, jelly beans, or Cheerios.

Randomly call out the sounds of the phonograms. For instance, for the letter y̱, ask your student to place a jelly bean over the letter that can say /y/–/ĭ/–/ī/–/ē/.

As you call each sound or group of sounds, your student should put a marker over the corresponding letter. When your student has filled all six of the trucks, he can say "Dump it!"

Lesson 48: Additional Sounds for E, U, Y, and CH

Read-Aloud Time   Read a Story or Poem

Read aloud to your student for twenty minutes.

Track Your Progress

Mark the Progress Chart

Have your student mark Lesson 48 on the Progress Chart.

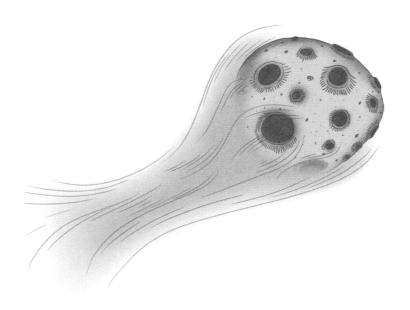

Lesson 48: Additional Sounds for E, U, Y, and CH

Lesson 49 - Read "The Sled" and "Ducks in a Truck"

In this lesson, students will read two short stories, and use the Table of Contents to locate information.

You will need: ☐ *Blast Off to Reading!* pages 313-318

☐ *Cobweb the Cat* book

☐ Optional: *The Runt Pig* book

Review

Review the Phonogram Cards that are behind the Review divider in your student's Reading Review Box. Show the card to your student and have him say the sound(s). If necessary, remind your student of the sound(s).

Review the Word Cards that are behind the Review divider in your student's Reading Review Box. If your student has difficulty reading the word, build the word with letter tiles and have your student sound it out using the procedure shown in Appendix C: Full Blending Procedure.

New Teaching

Story 1: "The Sled"

Complete Activity Sheet

"Sometimes when you need something but can't get it, you have to be creative and improvise. In this activity, you'll use your creativity to solve problems."

Make It Work!

Remove pages 313-315 from the *Blast Off* activity book.

Cut out the cards and spread them on the table.

Read the "problem prompts" below to your student one at a time. Each time, your student should look at the cards and find a solution to the problem.

New Teaching
(continued)

For example, you might ask, "What would you do if you were really thirsty but the water wasn't working?" Your student might choose ice cubes and say, "I would suck on ice cubes," or the bike and say, "I would ride my bike to my friend's house," or the phone and say, "I'd call my grandma." There are no wrong answers as long as the student can defend his choices.

<u>Problem prompts</u>

What would you do if you were really thirsty but the water wasn't working at your house?

What would you do if your friend needed to be cheered up?

What would you do if you were cold?

What could you use if you wanted to make a musical instrument?

What would you do if you got caught in the rain?

What could you use if you wanted to make a fort in the backyard?

What could you use if you wanted to make a costume?

Read the Warm-Up Sheet for "The Sled"

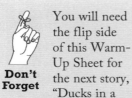

Don't Forget
You will need the flip side of this Warm-Up Sheet for the next story, "Ducks in a Truck." If you won't be completing that portion of the lesson today, return this Warm-Up Sheet to the activity book for safe keeping.

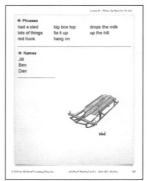

Remove page 317 from the activity book.

Have your student practice reading words and phrases that will be encountered in "The Sled."

Optional: Use the Table of Contents

If you still have *The Runt Pig* book handy, you may wish to include this optional discussion.

"Turn to the table of contents in *The Runt Pig* book." Help your student locate the table of contents.

"In the table of contents, find the story called 'Fun at the Pond' that you read several weeks ago, and then turn to that page." Student turns to page 179.

"Flip through this story and tell me the names of the three children." *Jill, Dan, and Ben.*

"What season is it in the story?" *Summer (or other reasonable answer).*

New Teaching
(continued)

"Now, turn to page 121 of *Cobweb the Cat*. The same children appear in this next story, 'The Sled.' Flip through the first few pages. What season is it in this story?" *Winter.*

Teach Vocabulary and Activate Prior Knowledge

Drop a book on the table and ask the student to describe the sound. "When something heavy falls, we often use the word *thud* to describe the sound. What other words could we use to describe the sound?" *Possible answers: smash, boom, crash.*

"In our next story, something—or someone—goes *thud!*"

"Have you ever been sledding in the snow? If you didn't have a real sled, what do you think you could use to slide down a hill?" Discuss your student's ideas.

"Let's see what the children in this story do when they can't find a sled."

Read "The Sled"

"Turn to page 121 in your reader and read 'The Sled' aloud." Discuss your student's ideas for the questions below as you come to them.

After page 125: "Look at the illustration. Do you see anything in the picture that could be a sled?"

After page 129: "What do you think will happen if they hit that bump?"

New Teaching
(continued)

Story 2: "Ducks in a Truck"

Read the Warm-Up Sheet for "Ducks in a Truck"

Remove page 318 from the activity book.

Have your student practice reading words and phrases that will be encountered in "Ducks in a Truck."

Teach Vocabulary and Activate Prior Knowledge

Point out the illustration of quills on the Warm-Up Sheet. "*Quills* are the hollow, sharp spines of animals like porcupines and hedgehogs. If you threaten a porcupine, he may bristle his quills at you!"

Point out the illustration of a dock on the Warm-Up Sheet. "A *dock* is a platform that juts into the water. People tie their boats to the dock to make it easier to get in and out."

"Have you ever heard the saying *a picture is worth a thousand words*? What do you think it means?" If necessary, explain that it means you can often understand more from a single picture than you can from many words.

"In this next story, a flock of ducks gets into all sorts of trouble while out riding in a truck. The text doesn't tell us the whole story. You have to look at the pictures to see what really happens. The pictures are worth a thousand words."

Read "Ducks in a Truck"

"Turn to page 137 in your reader and read 'Ducks in a Truck' aloud." Discuss your student's ideas for the questions below as you come to them.

After page 138: "Where are the ducks going in their truck? Look at the illustration for clues."

New Teaching
(continued)

After page 139: "Can you tell what happened to the duck with the bump? Look at the illustration for clues." *He fell off the truck and bumped his head when they hit a rock.*

After reading: "Although the story doesn't come out and say exactly what happens to each duck, the illustrations give you clues."

Have your student look at the illustrations on the following pages and answer the questions.

"Look at page 141. What happens after the duck gets stuck with quills?" *The truck driver takes all the quills out and puts band-aids on the duck.*

"Look at page 145. What happens to the duck as they pass the snakes?" *A snake wraps itself around his neck like a scarf.*

"Look at pages 147. What happens to the duck who goes on the dock?" *He gets a kiss from a duck on the dock.*

Read-Aloud Time

Read a Story or Poem

Read aloud to your student for twenty minutes.

Track Your Progress

Mark the Progress Chart

Have your student mark Lesson 49 on the Progress Chart.

A big astral woof to you,
space friend!

I was just thinking how far we've come
in these 49 lessons—and we're almost done!
What's been your favorite part?
I like the activity sheets. So far we've ...

fed word bones to a monster
had lunch with a yak
saved a bug from terrible dangers
made a slop pie
ridden trains, trucks, and horses
investigated facts

That's a lot of adventure, but nothing two
SPACEDOGS, MASTERS OF THE UNIVERSE
can't handle!

ONWARD!

Lesson 49: Read "The Sled" and "Ducks in a Truck"

Lesson 50 - Short Vowels and Counting Syllables

This lesson will teach the term *short vowel sounds* and how to count syllables.

You will need: ☐ Letter tiles <u>a</u>, <u>e</u>, <u>i</u>, <u>o</u>, and <u>u</u>

☐ *Blast Off to Reading!* pages 319-322

Before You Begin

Preview Short Vowels

In this lesson, your student will be introduced to the concept that vowels have a short sound. Very simply, a vowel's short sound is its first sound: /ă/ as in *hat*, /ĕ/ as in *beg*, /ĭ/ as in *sit*, /ŏ/ as in *not*, and /ŭ/ as in *hug*.

So far, your student hasn't needed to know the term *short vowel* to decode words because all the words your student has been asked to decode have contained short vowels. But now we are preparing to decode words in which the vowel appears at the end of a syllable and is therefore long, as in *be*, *hi*, and *go*, which are taught in Lesson 52. Being familiar with the terms *short vowel* and *long vowel* will enable your student to recognize the difference and become a stronger reader.

Preview Counting Syllables

Words are made up of syllables. A word may have one, two, or even more syllables. The number of vowel sounds in a word determines the number of syllables. For example:

- *bat* has one vowel sound and therefore one syllable
- *sticky* has two vowel sounds and therefore two syllables
- *south* has one vowel sound—/ow/—and therefore one syllable

Fortunately, there is an easy way to recognize and count syllables: by clapping. In this lesson, you will demonstrate how to clap syllables and then provide practice for your student. For example:

- *puppy* has two syllables: *pup* [clap]–*py* [clap]
- *tape* has one syllable: *tape* [clap]

The clapping method works well with most students, but see Appendix K if you need alternative methods.

<table>
<tr>
<td>Before You Begin
(continued)</td>
<td></td>
<td>If you are using Reading Games with Ziggy the Zebra, you can play "Blast Off with Ziggy" for additional practice with counting syllables.</td>
</tr>
</table>

Review

Review the Phonogram Cards that are behind the Review divider in your student's Reading Review Box. Show the card to your student and have him say the sound. If necessary, remind your student of the sound.

Review the Word Cards that are behind the Review divider in your student's Reading Review Box. If your student has difficulty reading the word, build the word with letter tiles and have your student sound it out using the procedure shown in Appendix C: Full Blending Procedure.

New Teaching

Teach Short Vowel Sounds

Put the letter tiles <u>a</u>, <u>e</u>, <u>i</u>, <u>o</u>, and <u>u</u> in front of your student.

Point to the <u>a</u> tile.   a

"Tell me the three sounds of this letter." /ă/–/ā/–/ah/.

"Which of those sounds is the first sound?" /ă/.

"Good. The first sound you said, /ă/, is called the **short sound of <u>a</u>**."

Point to the <u>e</u> tile.   e

"What sounds does this letter make?" /ĕ/–/ē/.

"Good. The first sound you said, /ĕ/, is called the **short sound of <u>e</u>**."

Repeat this activity with letter tiles <u>i</u>, <u>o</u>, and <u>u</u> so your student can see that the first sound is the short sound.

Lesson 50: Short Vowels and Counting Syllables

New Teaching
(continued)

Counting Syllables

In this next exercise, you will demonstrate what a syllable is by clapping your hands as you say the syllables.

"All words have syllables. A word might have one, two, or even more syllables."

"*Swimming* has two syllables: *swim* [clap]–*ing* [clap]."
"*Grass* has one syllable: *grass* [clap]."
"*Reindeer* has two syllables: *rein* [clap]–*deer* [clap]."

"Now you try. Clap your hands for each syllable in the word *dog*."

Have your student practice with the following words.

| ham | telephone | sixteen | grape | table |
| butterfly | ring | zipper | tent | purple |

Complete Activity Sheet

Cute Critters
Remove pages 319-322 from the *Blast Off* activity book.

Cut out all the cards. Mix them up and lay them on the table with the illustrations facing up.

Lay out the numbers 1, 2, and 3, which represent the possible numbers of syllables. Have your student sort the cards into three piles according to the number of syllables in the animals' names.

Read-Aloud Time Read a Story or Poem

Read aloud to your student for twenty minutes.

Track Your Progress

Mark the Progress Chart

Have your student mark Lesson 50 on the Progress Chart.

Lesson 50: Short Vowels and Counting Syllables

Lesson 51 - Read "Biff and the Bathtub" and "The Wind on the Hill"

In this lesson, students will read two short stories and draw a character picture from oral instructions.

You will need: ☐ *Blast Off to Reading!* pages 323-326

☐ *Cobweb the Cat* book ☐ piece of paper to draw on

Review

Review the Phonogram Cards that are behind the Review divider in your student's Reading Review Box. Show the card to your student and have him say the sound(s). If necessary, remind your student of the sound(s).

Review the Word Cards that are behind the Review divider in your student's Reading Review Box. If your student has difficulty reading the word, build the word with letter tiles and have your student sound it out using the procedure shown in Appendix C: Full Blending Procedure.

New Teaching

Story 1: "Biff and the Bathtub"

Complete Activity Sheet

"In our next story, you will meet Biff, a strange-looking creature. Let's see if you can guess what Biff will look like and draw your own version."

Monster Draw

Remove page 323 from the *Blast Off* activity book and set it aside.

Give your student a blank piece of paper to draw on. Read the following descriptions one by one and have your student draw his version of Biff based on these descriptions.

- Biff has a round face.
- Biff has big eyes and a big smile.
- Biff has sharp claws.
- Biff is covered in fur.
- Biff has a long tail.
- Biff has some sharp teeth.

New Teaching
(continued)

When your student is done with his drawing, have him cut around his monster and place it in the tub illustration provided.

Read the Warm-Up Sheet for "Biff and the Bathtub"

Don't Forget You will need the flip side of this Warm-Up Sheet for the next story, "The Wind on the Hill." If you won't be completing that portion of the lesson today, return this Warm-Up Sheet to the activity book for safekeeping.

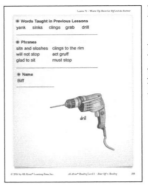

Remove page 325 from the activity book.

Have your student practice reading words and phrases that will be encountered in "Biff and the Bathtub."

Teach Vocabulary and Activate Prior Knowledge

Point out the illustration of a drill on the Warm-Up Sheet. "A *drill* is a tool for making holes in wood, cement, metal, and other materials."

"What would you do if you found Biff in your bathtub? How would you get him out?"

"In the story, the narrator tells us to act gruff with Biff. *Gruff* means rough and firm, so if you act gruff with Biff, you're showing him who's the boss! What is the opposite of gruff?" *Possible answers: friendly, cheerful, polite.*

"Let's see how the child in this story gets Biff out of the bathtub."

Read "Biff and the Bathtub"

"Turn to page 153 in your reader and read 'Biff and the Bathtub' aloud." Discuss your student's ideas for the questions below as you come to them.

After page 155: "How do you think Biff got in the bathtub in the first place? Where do you think he came from?"

New Teaching
(continued)

After page 161: "Why do you think the narrator grabs a drill? What does he hope will happen?"

After reading: "Does your picture look like Biff? How would you describe Biff?"

Story 2: "The Wind on the Hill"

Read the Warm-Up Sheet for "The Wind on the Hill"

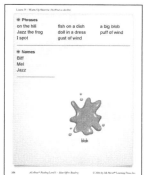

Remove page 326 from the activity book.

Have your student practice reading words and phrases that will be encountered in "The Wind on the Hill."

Point out the name *Mel* in the Names section. "Mel is a nickname for Melanie."

Teach Vocabulary and Activate Prior Knowledge

Point out the illustration of a blob on the Warm-Up Sheet. "A *blob* is a large object that doesn't have a distinct shape. If you say something looks like a blob, it means you can't really tell what it is."

"Sometimes clouds look like big blobs, and other times they make interesting shapes in the sky. Have you ever looked up at the clouds and imagined that they formed an animal shape or something other than a cloud?" Discuss your student's ideas about clouds.

"In this next story, a boy and a girl see lots of things in the clouds."

New Teaching
(continued)

Read "The Wind on the Hill"

"Turn to page 165 in your reader and read 'The Wind on the Hill' aloud." Discuss your student's ideas for the questions below as you come to them.

After pages 174-175: "What do you see in the clouds on these pages?"

After page 176: "Why do Greg and Mel run away at the end?"

Read-Aloud Time

Read a Story or Poem

Read aloud to your student for twenty minutes.

Track Your Progress

Mark the Progress Chart

Have your student mark Lesson 51 on the Progress Chart.

Lesson 52 - Open and Closed Syllables

This lesson will teach long vowel sounds, the concept of open and closed syllables, and words containing open syllables.

You will need: ☐ Letter tiles <u>a</u>, <u>e</u>, <u>i</u>, <u>o</u>, and <u>u</u>   ☐ Word Cards 186-193
☐ *Blast Off to Reading!* pages 327-334

Before You Begin

This is the final "new concept" lesson in Level 1!

Preview Long Vowel Sounds

In Lesson 50, your student learned that the first sound of a vowel is its short sound. Today your student will learn that the second sound of a vowel is its long sound. When a vowel says its long sound, it says its name. For example:

- the long sound of <u>a</u> is /ā/
- the long sound of <u>e</u> is /ē/

Preview Open and Closed Syllables

The letter tiles make it easy to teach the difference between open and closed syllables.

sh e d

In the word *shed*, the vowel <u>e</u> is "closed in" by a consonant. When a vowel is in a closed syllable, it usually says its short sound.

Now watch what happens when we remove the consonant from the end of the word.

sh e

The vowel <u>e</u> is now "open." There is nothing closing it in. When a vowel is in an open syllable, it usually says its long sound. That's why <u>e</u> says /ē/ in this word.

Review

Review the Phonogram Cards that are behind the Review divider in your student's Reading Review Box. Show the card to your student and have him say the sound. If necessary, remind your student of the sound.

Review the Word Cards that are behind the Review divider in your student's Reading Review Box. If your student has difficulty reading the word, build the word with letter tiles and have your student sound it out using the procedure shown in Appendix C: Full Blending Procedure.

One at a time, point to the letter tiles <u>a</u>, <u>e</u>, <u>i</u>, <u>o</u>, and <u>u</u>. Have your student tell you the short vowel sound of each letter.

New Teaching

Teach Long Vowel Sounds

Put the letter tiles <u>a</u>, <u>e</u>, <u>i</u>, <u>o</u>, and <u>u</u> in front of your student.

Point to the <u>a</u> tile.　a

"Tell me the three sounds of this letter." /ă/–/ā/–/ah/.

"Which of those sounds is the **short** sound?" /ă/ (or *the first sound*).

"Good. The first sound of a vowel is its short sound. We also have a name for the **second** sound of a vowel. The second sound is called its **long** sound."

"What is the second sound of the letter <u>a</u>?" /ā/.

Point to the <u>e</u> tile.　e

"What are the two sounds of this letter?" /ĕ/–/ē/.

"What is the long sound of this letter?" /ē/.

Point to the <u>i</u> tile.　i

"What are the three sounds of this letter?" /ĭ/–/ī/–/ē/.

"What is the long sound of this letter?" /ī/.

Lesson 52: Open and Closed Syllables

New Teaching
(continued)

Point to the o̲ tile.

Your student can probably see the pattern now.

"And what do you think the long sound of o̲ is?" /ō/.

"And the long sound of u̲ is?" /ū/. 　u

"Good. The long sound of a letter is the same as its name."

Teach Closed and Open Syllables

Build the word *shed*. 　sh　e　d

"What is this word?" *Shed.*

"Point to the vowel." *Student points to the e̲.*

"Is there anything after the e̲?" *Yes, d̲.*

"Good. We say that the e̲ is closed in by the d̲. We call this a **closed** syllable."

"Is the vowel in *shed* short or long?" *Short.*

"Right. When a vowel is in a **closed** syllable, it usually says its **short** sound."

Remove the d̲ tile. 　sh　e

"Is there anything after the e̲ now?" *No.*

"We can say that the e̲ is **open**, because there is nothing closing it in."

"When a vowel is in an **open** syllable, it usually says its **long** sound."

Point to the e̲. "What does the e̲ say in this word?" /ē/.

"What is this word?" *She.*

New Teaching
(continued)

Build the following words. Have your student tell you whether the syllable is **open** or **closed**.

he	*Open.*
hem	*Closed.*
so	*Open.*
sock	*Closed.*
got	*Closed.*

For additional practice, use the following words.

go	**wet**	**we**	**no**	**not**
I	**it**	**bed**	**be**	

Practice Reading Words

Have your student practice reading the words on Word Cards 186-193.

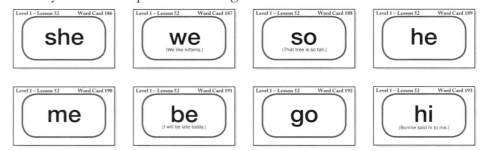

File the Word Cards behind the Review divider of the Reading Review Box.

Complete Activity Sheet

Spaceships
Remove pages 327-331 from the *Blast Off* activity book.

Color the spaceships and the astronauts, if desired. Cut out the ships and astronauts.

Place the nine astronauts in a group with the words facing down and mix them up.

Have your student select an astronaut, read the word aloud, and then decide whether the syllable is open or closed. If the syllable is open, he can

Lesson 52: Open and Closed Syllables

New Teaching
(continued)

place the astronaut on the spaceship with the open door. If the syllable is closed, he can place the astronaut on the spaceship with the closed door. Repeat until all the astronauts are correctly placed.

Practice Fluency

Remove pages 333-334 from the activity book.

Have your student read from the Practice Sheet.

Read-Aloud Time   Read a Story or Poem

Read aloud to your student for twenty minutes.

Track Your Progress   Mark the Progress Chart

Have your student mark Lesson 52 on the Progress Chart.

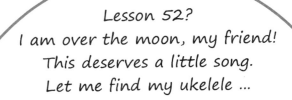

Lesson 52?
I am over the moon, my friend!
This deserves a little song.
Let me find my ukelele ...

AHEM.

I see stardust in your hair—
you're almost there, almost there.
One quick ride on a comet tail—
you've blazed a trail, blazed a trail.
Just make a left at Success Star—
and there you are, there you are:
finished, over, out, and DONE
with Level 1, Level 1!

Can I get a WOOF?!

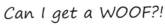

Lesson 52: Open and Closed Syllables

Lesson 53 - Read "Gus and Hal Go on a Trip" and "The Best Lunch"

In this lesson, students will read two short stories that give them practice with open syllables, and complete a story sequencing activity.

You will need: ☐ *Blast Off to Reading!* pages 335-339

☐ *Cobweb the Cat* book

Before You Begin

This is the final story lesson! These last two stories pull together all the concepts taught in Level 1, including the newly learned open syllable words.

Enjoy the stories—and perhaps plan a little celebration!

Review

Review the Phonogram Cards that are behind the Review divider in your student's Reading Review Box. Show the card to your student and have him say the sound(s). If necessary, remind your student of the sound(s).

Review the Word Cards that are behind the Review divider in your student's Reading Review Box. If your student has difficulty reading the word, build the word with letter tiles and have your student sound it out using the procedure shown in Appendix C: Full Blending Procedure.

a b c Review short and long vowels. One at a time, point to the letter tiles <u>a</u>, <u>e</u>, <u>i</u>, <u>o</u>, and <u>u</u>. Have your student tell you the short sound of each letter. Then have him tell you the long sound of each letter.

Review closed and open syllables. Build the word *met*. "Is this an open or closed syllable?" *Closed.*

Remove the <u>t</u>. "Is this an open or closed syllable?" *Open.*

Repeat with the words *bet, go, not, he, shell, she.*

New Teaching

Read the Warm-Up Sheet for "Gus and Hal Go on a Trip"

Remove page 335 from the *Blast Off* activity book.

Have your student practice reading words and phrases that will be encountered in "Gus and Hal Go on a Trip."

Teach Vocabulary and Activate Prior Knowledge

Point out the illustration of chopsticks on the Warm-Up Sheet. "These are *chopsticks*. Chopsticks are thin sticks of wood that are held together in one hand and used as eating utensils, like we use forks. Chopsticks are often used in China and Japan."

"In the next story, the characters go on an adventure. One character calls it a *thrill*. If something is a thrill, it is exciting and gives you a great feeling inside. If you love puppies and you get to babysit for a new litter of puppies, that would be a thrill for you. If you love fast bikes and you get to ride down a steep hill, that would be a thrill for you."

"What is a thrill for one person might not be a thrill for another person. If your friend is afraid of dogs, babysitting for a litter of puppies wouldn't be a thrill. If your sister doesn't like fast bikes, riding down a steep hill wouldn't be a thrill—it would be scary."

"What is something that is a thrill for you?"

"If you could go on an adventure, where would you go and what would you do?"

"If you could only take one thing with you to eat, what would it be?"

"Let's see what happens when the chipmunks in this story go on an adventure."

In *The Lost List* …	Yes	No
Did Finn drop the list?		NO
Did the list get lost?		NO
Did Finn get the things Mom had on the list?		NO
Was Mom mad at Finn?	Yes	
Did Finn get buns?	Yes	
Did Finn get fish?		NO

All About® Reading Level 1 – *Blast Off to Reading*

All About® Reading Level 1 − *Blast Off to Reading*

● Phrases

shop for lunch	hot cross buns	check the list
glad to help	bag of gumdrops	things for lunch
gust of wind	pass the jam	sip of pop
got lost	lots of stuff	

● Name

Finn

hot cross buns

All About® Reading Level 1 – *Blast Off to Reading*

New Teaching
(continued)

Read "Gus and Hal Go on a Trip"

"Turn to page 179 in your reader and read 'Gus and Hal Go on a Trip' aloud." Discuss your student's ideas for the questions below as you come to them.

After page 184: "Gus and Hal have different reactions to hitting a rock. Why is Gus happy? Why is Hal worried?"

After page 187: "Look at the illustrations on pages 186 and 187. Which pieces of junk did they use to create the Muck Bus?"

After page 190: "How do you think a stick of gum can help?"

After reading: "Do you think these chipmunks have anything in common with the kids in the story 'The Sled'? *Possible answer: They also solve problems by finding ways to use objects in new ways.*

Complete Activity Sheet

"Gus and Hal made several vehicles out of the lunch box. Let's see if you remember the order in which they made these vehicles."

All Aboard!
Remove pages 337-338 from the activity book.

Cut out the three vehicle cards and mix them up.

Have your student put the cards in the order that they appeared in the story. He may refer to the story if necessary.

Story 2: "The Best Lunch"

Read the Warm-Up Sheet for "The Best Lunch"

Remove page 339 from the activity book.

Have your student practice reading words and phrases that will be encountered in "The Best Lunch."

Teach Vocabulary and Activate Prior Knowledge

Point out the illustration of a giraffe on the Warm-Up Sheet. "This is a *giraffe*. A giraffe is a large African mammal with a very long neck. It is the tallest living animal."

Point out the illustration of Swiss cheese on the Warm-Up Sheet. "*Swiss* is a type of yellow cheese that usually has large holes in it. Swiss cheese originally came from Switzerland."

"What is your favorite kind of cheese? What would the best lunch include for you?"

"What if you didn't have one of those ingredients for your best lunch? What would you do?"

"The animals in this story get very creative to make the best lunch. Let's see what they do."

Read "The Best Lunch"

"Turn to page 197 in your reader and read 'The Best Lunch' aloud." Discuss your student's ideas for the questions below as you come to them.

After page 207: "So far, five animals have added to the lunch. Who do you think will end up getting to eat the lunch?"

New Teaching
(continued)

After reading: "Look at the illustration on page 211. What do you think all the other animals are thinking?"

"Does this sound like a good lunch to you? Why or why not?"

Read-Aloud Time

Read a Story or Poem

Read aloud to your student for twenty minutes.

Track Your Progress

Mark the Progress Chart

Have your student mark Lesson 53 on the Progress Chart.

Celebrate!

Present Your Student with the Certificate of Achievement

What's Next?

All About Reading Level 1 gave your student extensive practice with short vowel words, and ended with a brief introduction to words with long vowel sounds. Level 2 will pick up from here, providing your student with much more practice and review of the long vowel sounds and open syllable types.

If your student has basic handwriting skills, this is also the perfect time to begin spelling instruction with *All About Spelling* Level 1, which will reinforce the phonograms and decoding skills that your student has learned so far, using the familiar multisensory approach.

Treat reading and spelling as two separate programs, and let your student work through the two subjects at his own pace. Most students move much more quickly through the reading program than through the spelling program since spelling is a more difficult skill.

SHA-ZAM!
You did it, space buddy! You've taken off and zoomed to the highest star.
I couldn't be prouder!

Thank you for sharing this space adventure with me. I know you'll use your new knowledge to explore the vast galaxies of reading goodness that stretch before you.

Now it's time to ...
BLAST OFF
to the next frontier!

3
Appendices

APPENDIX A
Scope and Sequence of Level 1

Your Student Will:	Lesson
Learn the blending procedure and the sounds of letters m̲, s̲, p̲, and a̲	1
Learn the sounds of phonograms n̲, t̲, b̲, and j̲ and the Leap Word the	2
Read a short story and learn about periods and exclamation points	3
Learn the sounds of phonograms g̲, d̲, c̲, and y̲ and that every word has a vowel	4
Read a short story and learn words with two meanings	5
Learn the sounds of phonograms h̲, k̲, and r̲ and the Leap Word a̲	6
Read two short stories and complete a comprehension activity	7
Learn the sounds of phonograms i̲, v̲, f̲, and z̲	8
Read two short stories and practice punctuation marks	9
Learn the sounds of phonograms o̲, l̲, and w̲ and the Leap Word of	10
Read two short stories and complete a comprehension activity	11
Learn the sound of phonogram u̲ and the second sound of s̲	12
Read two short stories and discuss a character's point of view	13
Learn the sound of phonogram e̲	14
Read two short stories and complete a story sequencing activity	15
Learn the sounds of phonograms qu̲ and x̲	16
Read two short stories and create silly sentences	17
Learn the concept of consonant teams and both sounds of consonant team th̲	18
Read two short stories and discuss character motivation	19
Learn the sound of consonant team sh̲	20
Read two short stories and discuss story setting	21
Learn the first sound of consonant team ch̲	22
Read two short stories and use illustrations to retell a story	23
Learn words with final blends and the Leap Word was	24
Read two short stories and match text with illustrations	25
Learn words with initial blends and the Leap Word to	26
Read two short stories and learn about onomatopoeia	27
Read two short stories and practice reading words with blends	28
Learn words ending in ff̲, ll̲, and ss̲ and the Leap Words said and I	29
Read two short stories and follow recipe instructions	30
Learn the Leap Words or, for, and no	31
Read two short stories and practice previously taught concepts	32
Read two short stories and discuss the main conflict	33

Your Student Will:	Lesson
Learn the sound of consonant team <u>ck</u>	34
Read two short stories and discuss character traits	35
Learn the sound of consonant team <u>ng</u>	36
Read two short stories and learn about the five senses in literature	37
Learn the sound of consonant team <u>nk</u>	38
Read two short stories and learn about cause and effect	39
Learn compound words and the Leap Word <u>do</u>	40
Read two short stories and discuss realism vs. fantasy	41
Learn plural words and verbs ending in <u>s</u> and <u>es</u>	42
Read two short stories and learn about rhyme	43
Learn additional sounds of phonograms <u>a</u>, <u>i</u>, and <u>c</u>	44
Read two short stories and skim text to answer questions	45
Learn additional sounds of phonograms <u>o</u> and <u>g</u>	46
Read two short stories and discuss character motivation	47
Learn additional sounds of phonograms <u>e</u>, <u>u</u>, <u>y</u>, and <u>ch</u>	48
Read two short stories and use the Table of Contents to locate information	49
Learn the term <u>short vowels</u> and learn to count syllables	50
Read two short stories and draw a character from oral instructions	51
Learn long vowel sounds and open and closed syllables	52
Read two short stories and complete a story sequencing activity	53

Appendix A: Scope and Sequence of Level 1

APPENDIX B
Phonograms Taught in Levels 1-4

Phonograms are letters or letter combinations that represent a single sound. For example, the letter b represents the sound /b/, as in *bat*. The letter combination sh represents the sound /sh/, as in *ship*.

Card #	Phonogram	Sound	For the Teacher's Use Only (example of word containing the phonogram)				Lesson/ Level
			Phonograms Taught in Level 1				**Lesson**
1	m	/m/	moon				1
2	s	/s/–/z/	sun	has			1, 12
3	p	/p/	pig				1
4	a	/ă/–/ā/–/ah/	apple	acorn	father		1, 44
5	n	/n/	nest				2
6	t	/t/	tent				2
7	b	/b/	bat				2
8	j	/j/	jam				2
9	g	/g/–/j/	goose	gem			4, 46
10	d	/d/	deer				4
11	c	/k/–/s/	cow	city			4, 44
12	y	/y/–/ĭ/–/ī/–/ē/	yarn	gym	my	happy	4, 48
13	h	/h/	hat				6
14	k	/k/	kite				6
15	r	/r/	rake				6
16	i	/ĭ/–/ī/–/ē/	itchy	ivy	radio		8, 44
17	v	/v/	vase				8
18	f	/f/	fish				8
19	z	/z/	zipper				8
20	o	/ŏ/–/ō/–/o͞o/–/ŭ/	otter	open	to	oven	10, 46
21	l	/l/	leaf				10
22	w	/w/	wave				10
23	u	/ŭ/–/ū/–/o͞o/	udder	unit	put		12, 48
24	e	/ĕ/–/ē/	echo	even			14, 48
25	qu	/kw/	queen				16
26	x	/ks/	ax				16

Card #	Phonogram	Sound	For the Teacher's Use Only (example of word containing the phonogram)	Lesson/ Level
27	th	/th/–/t̶h̶/	three then	18
28	sh	/sh/	ship	20
29	ch	/ch/–/k/–/sh/	child school chef	22, 48
30	ck	/k/, two-letter /k/	duck	34
31	ng	/ng/	king	36
32	nk	/ngk/	thank	38
Phonograms Taught in Level 2				
33	wh	/hw/	while	
34	ee	/ē/, double e	feed	
35	er	/er/ as in *her*	her	
36	ar	/ar/	car	
37	or	/or/–/er/ as in *work*	corn work	
38	ed	/ĕd/–/d/–/t/	wanted snowed dropped	
39	oy	/oy/ that we **may** use at the end of English words	toy	Level 2
40	oi	/oy/ that we may **not** use at the end of English words	oil	
41	aw	/aw/ that we **may** use at the end of English words	saw	
42	au	/aw/ that we may **not** use at the end of English words	haul	
43	ow	/ow/–/ō/	cow low	
44	ou	/ow/–/ō/–/o͞o/–/ŭ/	mouse soul soup touch	
Phonograms Taught in Level 3				
45	ai	/ā/, two-letter /ā/ that we may **not** use at the end of English words	rain	
46	ay	ā/, two-letter /ā/ that we **may** use at the end of English words	day	Level 3
47	oa	/ō/, two-letter /ō/ that we may **not** use at the end of English words	boat	
48	ir	/er/ as in *first*	first	

Appendix B: Phonograms Taught in Levels 1-4

Card #	Phonogram	Sound	For the Teacher's Use Only (example of word containing the phonogram)			Lesson/Level
49	ur	/er/ as in *nurse*	nurse			
50	oo	/o͞o/–/o͝o/–/ō/	food	book	floor	
51	ea	/ē/–/ĕ/–/ā/	leaf	bread	great	
52	igh	/ī/, three-letter /ī/	light			
53	tch	/ch/, three-letter /ch/	watch			
54	dge	/j/, three-letter /j/	badge			
55	ew	/o͞o/–/ū/	grew	few		Level 3
56	wr	/r/, two-letter /r/ used only at the beginning of a word	write			
57	kn	/n/, two-letter /n/ used only at the beginning of a word	know			
58	eigh	/ā/, four-letter /ā/	eight			
59	oe	/ō/, two-letter /ō/ that we **may** use at the end of English words	toe			
60	ti	/sh/, tall-letter /sh/	nation			
Phonograms Taught in Level 4						
61	ey	/ē/–/ā/	key	they		
62	ear	/er/ as in *early*	early			
63	ui	/o͞o/	fruit			
64	ie	/ē/–/ī/	field	pie		
65	ph	/f/, two-letter /f/	phone			
66	gu	/g/, two-letter /g/	guide			
67	gn	/n/, two-letter /n/ used at the beginning or end of a base word	gnat			Level 4
68	augh	/aw/, four-letter /aw/	daughter			
69	ei	/ā/–/ē/	vein	ceiling		
70	ough	/ō/–/o͞o/–/ŭff/– /ŏff/–/aw/–/ow/	though cough	through thought	rough bough	
71	si	/sh/–/zh/	mission	vision		
72	mb	/m/, two-letter /m/	lamb			

Card #	Phonogram	Sound	For the Teacher's Use Only (example of word containing the phonogram)	Lesson/ Level
73	our	/er/ as in *journey*	journey	
74	ci	/sh/, short-letter /sh/	special	Level 4
75	rh	/r/, two-letter /r/ used in Greek words	rhyme	

Appendix B: Phonograms Taught in Levels 1-4

APPENDIX C
Full Blending Procedure

Decoding one-syllable words

1.   Build the word with letter tiles.   p a n

2.   Touch one letter at a time, and say the sound of each letter.

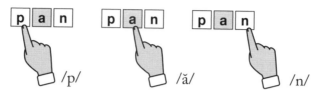

3.   Go back to the beginning of the word and blend the first two sounds together.

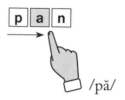

4.   Start at the beginning of the word again. Slide your finger under the letters and say the word slowly.

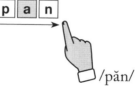

> Starting over at the beginning of the word is optional. Some students need the extra support provided by this step, while others do not.
>
> Whenever you feel that your student is ready, blend all three letters without this additional step.

5.   Finally, say the word at a normal pace, as we do when we speak.

> **"Touch the Vowel" Technique**
> Many errors in sounding out words are related to the vowel. If your student says the wrong vowel sound, ask him to touch the vowel and say the vowel sound first. After he says the correct sound for the vowel, he should go back and sound out the word from the beginning.

In Level 2, the blending procedure will be expanded as shown below.

Blending multisyllabic words

1.   Build the word with letter tiles.

2.   Divide the word into syllables using the appropriate syllable division rules.

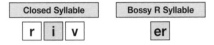

3.   Label the syllable types.

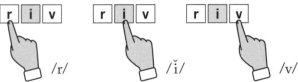

4.   Decode one syllable at a time, following the same procedure you would use for a one-syllable word.

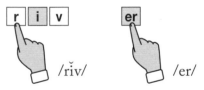

5.   Start at the beginning of the word again. Slide your finger under each syllable, saying the sound of the syllables.

6.   Finally, say the word at a normal pace, as we do when we speak.

      If the word has three or more syllables, follow the same procedure:
        1. Divide the word.
        2. Label the syllable types.
        3. Decode one syllable at a time.

Appendix C: Full Blending Procedure

APPENDIX D
Solving Letter Reversal Problems

Most of the letters of the alphabet have unique shapes, so no matter which way you turn them, they can't be confused with any other letters. For example, the letter <u>m</u> looks quite different from the letter <u>x</u>, and <u>f</u> is not likely to be confused with <u>z</u>.

There are a few notorious troublemakers, however, particularly <u>b</u> and <u>d</u>, the letters that students most often have trouble with.

It is easy to see where the confusion comes in: flip the <u>b</u> and it becomes a <u>d</u>. The beginning reader or dyslexic student may not realize that the direction of the letter matters, or he may not be able to remember which letter is which.

Letters and numbers that can be flipped include:

b d   p q   p d   n u   6 9

What is considered normal?

If your student is between the ages of three and seven, is just starting to read, and makes occasional reversal errors when reading or writing, it's perfectly normal. It doesn't mean that your student has dyslexia or a reading disability. Make a gentle correction and move on.

But if your student is eight years or older, has had prior reading instruction, and is making frequent letter reversal errors, it is important to take action to solve the reversal problems.

As reading instructors, we have two jobs to do regarding reversals:

1. Try to prevent confusion.
2. Where confusion exists, resolve it.

Try to prevent letter confusion before it begins.

The *All About Reading* program is carefully structured to minimize the likelihood of letter reversals. We teach the sounds of potentially confusing letters like <u>b</u> and <u>d</u> in separate lessons. The student's task is simplified because he only has to make one new visual discrimination at a time.

When your student is learning to print, be sure to teach correct letter formation. Doing so is critical to prevent confusion.

When forming the letter <u>b</u>, start with the stick first, followed by the circle. To write the letter <u>d</u>, start with the circle first, followed by the stick.

Have your student use lined paper so it is clear where the circle is in relation to the stick. Also be sure your student does not lift the pencil from the paper when writing any of the confusable letters.

What to do if your student already reverses letters.

If you are working with older learners, it may be too late to prevent confusion. They may have had a few false starts in reading, and may have already confused these troublemakers. They may encounter the letter <u>b</u> and misinterpret it as the letter <u>d</u>. They may read the word *bad* as *dab*, or *fad* as *fab*. You might give a gentle correction, pull out the corresponding Phonogram Cards, and re-teach the letters separately, but your student still mixes them up.

Below are four effective methods to clear up tough reversal problems.

The demonstrations are for correcting <u>b</u> and <u>d</u> reversals, but the same concepts can be applied to any letter or number. You may only need to use one of these methods, but for really resistant cases, you will need to use all four methods.

Please note that it's important to concentrate on just one letter per session. Wait until that letter is completely mastered before teaching another letter.

Method 1: Teach the letters <u>b</u> and <u>d</u> using tactile surfaces.

Have a variety of tactile surfaces for your student to choose from. Possibilities include flannel fabric, corrugated cardboard, very fine sandpaper, fluffy fur fabric, or a carpet square. Ask your student which surface reminds him of the letter <u>b</u>, and then cut a large lowercase <u>b</u> out of the chosen tactile surface.

Using the pointer finger of his dominant hand, have your student trace the letter <u>b</u> on the textured surface. Be sure that he starts and ends in the correct place. Practice until he can easily write the letter <u>b</u>.

When your student is ready to go on to a new letter, choose a different textured surface. If fine sandpaper was used for the letter <u>b</u>, perhaps furry fabric can be used for the letter <u>d</u>.

Method 2: Use "air writing" to reinforce proper letter formation.

Another simple but powerful method for correcting reversals is "air writing." Using the dominant hand, the student uses his entire arm to write letters in the air as he says the sound of the letter. The whole arm should be involved, and the student should pretend that his pointer finger is a pen.

Brain research shows that two ideas practiced at the same time can permanently bond the ideas together. In this case, the large movements of the arm combined with saying the sound of the letter helps link these two concepts together in your student's brain. Additionally, this multisensory activity takes advantage of the fact that the muscles in the shoulder and in the jaw have muscle memory, and this makes it easier for your student to recall the shape and sound of the letter.

Method #3: Teach the letters <u>b</u> and <u>d</u> using analogies.

Explain that the letter <u>b</u> is made up of two shapes: a bat and a ball. Using the tactile surface, demonstrate how you write the bat part of the letter first, followed by the ball.

As you write the letter <u>b</u>, say "bat-ball-/b/," like this:

To further clarify which side of the letter the straight line is on, tell your student that *first you grab the bat, then you hit the ball.*

Have your student practice this motion and chant many times over a two-minute time period. Repeat the exercise several times a day.

Show your student that when you are reading from left to right, you encounter the bat part of the letter first. If he is ever unsure of the sound this letter makes when he sees it, he should think to himself, "bat-ball-/b/." This will help him recall the sound of the letter <u>b</u>.

To teach the letter <u>d</u>, you can use the analogy of a doorknob and a door. The doorknob represents the circle part of the letter, and the door represents the straight line, like this:

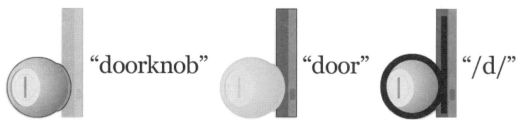

To clarify which side of the letter the straight line is on, tell your student that *first you grab the doorknob, then you open the door.*

Again, practice the motion and chant many times over a two-minute period. Repeat the exercise several times a day.

Show your student that when you are reading from left to right, you encounter the doorknob part of the letter first. If he is ever unsure of the sound this letter makes when he sees it, he should think to himself, "doorknob-door-/d/." He will now be able to recall the sound of the letter d.

Another common analogy to help with b and d is a bed. Though this analogy may help some kids, for others it may require more thought, and for many kids it may not become automatic.

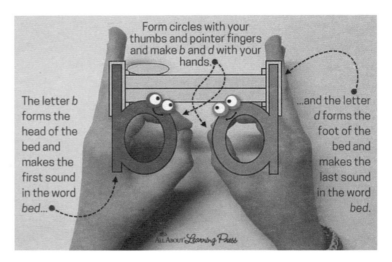

Method #4: Help your student notice the shape of our mouths while saying the letter sounds.

When we say /b/, our lips come together in a straight line. Point out that the straight line comes first when you write the letter b.

When we say /d/, our lips are open. Coincidentally, the circle comes first when you write the letter d.

If your student misreads a b as a d, refer back to the tactile surface activity and air writing that you did together. Point to the misread letter and say, *If you wrote this letter, what would this letter say?*

If your student can't answer easily, ask him to draw the letter b using air writing. The sound of the letter (/b/–bat) should come more easily this way. Then have your student read the word again.

APPENDIX E
How to Assemble Word Flippers

Word Flippers are a fun way for your student to practice fluency. Follow these steps to assemble and use them in your lessons.

1. Remove the appropriate pages from the activity book. Cut apart the pages on the dotted lines.

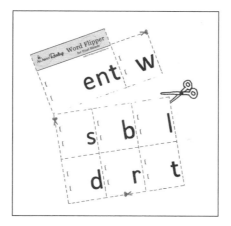

2. Put the larger pieces of paper on the bottom. Stack the smaller pieces on top. Note that some Word Flippers will be stacked on the left side and some on the right side.

3. Staple the Word Flipper along the left or right side, as indicated.

4. Have your student turn the pages and read the words that are formed.

APPENDIX F
Tips and Activities for Using the Practice Sheets

Fluency is the ability to read smoothly, accurately, and with expression, and the Practice Sheets are an important part of developing your student's fluency. But students don't always find the Practice Sheets as exciting as the other hands-on activities in the lessons.

If working on Practice Sheets becomes a chore for you and your student, try some of the following games and creative activities to make them fun again.

Be sure to photocopy the Practice Sheets before playing games that require the pages to be cut into strips or single words.

Games and Activities

- **Feed the monster.** Cut out the monster on page 324. Cut the Practice Sheets into strips. Have your student feed the strips to the monster as he reads them.

- **Cut up the Practice Sheets** and use the words and sentences with the games from the supplemental *Reading Games with Ziggy the Zebra.*

- **Number the rows** of words and sentences on the Practice Sheet 1-6, repeating those numbers as necessary. Have the student roll a die and read the words or sentence in the row of the number he rolled. For example, if he rolls a 2, he must read the words in row 2.

- **Read with a buddy.** Take turns reading lines with your student, or let her read with a favorite stuffed animal or toy.

- **Use sticker dots.** Break up the assignment and reduce your student's frustration by creating a "starting dot" and a "stopping dot."

- **Play hide and seek** with words and sentences. Cut up the practice sheets and hide the pieces around the room. When the student finds a piece, he must read it before searching for the next piece.

- **Use an online word search puzzle maker** to create your own word search puzzle using your student's review words. Have the student read the words as she finds them.

- **Have your student search for and read** only words that begin with a particular letter.

- **Play Swat the Words.** Find or make an object to use as a swatter, such as a new flyswatter, a plastic ruler, or even just your student's hand. Cut out words from the Practice Sheet and lay them out on the table. Have your student find and swat each word as you read it out loud. Then switch—you swat while your student reads.

- **Break up the Practice Sheet** by covering it with a piece of paper. Slide the paper down to uncover one line or section at a time.

- **Make progress more concrete.** Allow your student to track progress using colored highlighters or fun stickers.

Art and Creative Play

- **Let your student use the Ziggy puppet** to read the words and sentences on the Practice Sheets.

- **Make a word road.** Cut the rows of words into long strips. Place the strips on a long table or on the floor to make a road. Have your student drive a matchbox car over the words as he reads them.

- **Illustrate the words.** Select a few words and have your student draw a picture for each one. She may then make a collage of the words and pictures.

- **Silly sentences.** Have your student read a word and then make up a silly sentence using the word.

- **Have fun with emotions!** On separate pieces of scrap paper, draw some simple faces showing different emotions and moods like happy, sad, angry, scared, rude, lovestruck, worried, hopeful, and so on. Put the faces in a hat. Cut out the words and sentences from the Practice Sheet and put those in another hat. Have your student pick a word/sentence from one hat, pick a face from the other hat, and then ham it up by reading the word with the selected emotion.

Snacks and Rewards

- **Eat your words!** Motivate your student to read each row of the Practice Sheet by putting a chocolate chip, marshmallow, M&M, popcorn, granola, fruit, or other favorite treat at the end of a section or row. At the end of the practice session, snuggle up with a story and munch on the rest of the snack.

- **Set up a points system** in the corner of your white board or on a separate chart, and give your student a small prize when she reaches 100 points. For example, you might give your student one point for every correct word she can read in five minutes. You might combine the points system with Phonogram Card and Word Card review as well so your student has more chances to rack up points. There are many point variations, so use what works best for you.

Positive Words
Fluent reading is hard work for your student! Catch him working hard and give him a few words of encouragement. Try positive words like these:

- "Very good! You are a quick learner!"
- "Hey, you got that the first time!"
- "You are doing great!"
- "That was a tough one, and you got it!"
- "You remembered that from yesterday—great!"
- "I can tell that you tried hard to figure that out."

> **Tip!** Many of the tips and activities in Appendices F, G, and H can be mixed and matched to review Practice Sheets, Phonogram Cards, or Word Cards.

Feed the Monster

Instructions: Print the monster and cut a slit in its mouth. Cut your Practice Sheet into strips. Have your student read each strip aloud and "feed" it to the monster as it is completed.

Appendix F: Tips and Activities for Using the Practice Sheets

APPENDIX G
Activities for Reviewing Phonograms

Games and Activities

- **Practice phonograms** using the games from the supplemental *Reading Games with Ziggy the Zebra.*

- **Play Swat the Phonograms.** Find or make an object to use as a swatter, such as a new flyswatter, a plastic ruler, or even just your student's hand. Lay out a selection of Phonogram Cards on the table. Have your student find and swat each card as you say the sound(s) of the phonogram. Then switch—you swat while your student says the sound(s).

- **Play Phonogram Bingo.** Make a bingo card with a selection of review phonograms.

- **Play Phonogram Go Fish.** Choose 10-15 phonograms to practice. Use index cards to make up two identical sets of cards. Play according to the regular rules.

- **Play Phonogram Snowball Fight.** Write a selection of review phonograms on index cards and tape them to the wall. As you call out phonograms, have your student locate the phonogram on the wall, say the sound(s), and throw a snowball at it. Use ping-pong balls, nerf balls, styrofoam balls, or even crumpled paper for snowballs.

- **Jump on it!** Write a selection of review phonograms on index cards and spread them around the floor. Have your student locate and jump to the correct phonogram as you call out the sound(s).

- **Play Phonogram Hopscotch.** Write a different phonogram in each square of a hopscotch grid. Gather a different marker for each student, such as a beanbag, stone, or bottle cap. Follow the standard rules, but when the student stops to pick up his marker, he says the sound(s) of the phonogram in that square.

- **Play Phonogram Ball.** Use a marker to write phonograms on a large beach ball. Have the student throw the ball in the air, catch it, and then say the sound(s) of the phonograms closest to his thumbs.

Art and Creative Play

- **Stamp it.** If you have letter stamps, use them to reinforce the phonogram of the day. After teaching a phonogram, use the stamps to stamp the phonogram on the back of your student's hand. Refer to it throughout the day, asking what the phonogram is, what sound(s) it makes, and so on.

- **Color it.** Look for coloring book pages with big spaces and write review phonograms in those spaces. Have the student say the sound(s) of each phonogram. If she says the sound(s) correctly, she may color that space. Continue until the picture is complete.

- **Build a Phonogram Card city.** Create a city in your living room by arranging the Phonogram Cards face down on the floor and furniture so that every Phonogram Card is a building. Have your student drive around the city, saying the sound(s) of the phonograms as he arrives at each building. If he says the sound(s) correctly, turn that card face up. The game continues until all the cards have been turned face up.

Snacks and Rewards

- **Play Phonogram Cup Hunt.** Choose 5-7 review phonograms, write them on mailing labels, and attach the labels to plastic cups. Under one of the cups, place a small wrapped treat, like a few raisins or chocolate chips in plastic wrap, and then have your student close her eyes as you mix up the cups. Have your student open her eyes, choose a cup, say the sound(s) of the phonogram on the cup, and lift the cup. Continue playing until she finds the treat.

- **Play Snack Track.** Use the Phonogram Cards to make a snack track on your floor. Place a small snack next to each card. Starting at the beginning of the track, have your student hop forward one space and say the sound(s) of the phonogram. If he says the sound(s) correctly, he gets to eat the snack and advance to the next card. If incorrect, he must move back two spaces and try again.

- **Make an ABC Snack.** Go to the ABC Snacks link on the All About Learning Press blog at http://abc-snacks.com. Choose the phonogram you are working on and make a yummy snack for it.

Activities for Reviewing Word Cards

Games and Activities

- **Practice review words** using the games from the supplemental *Reading Games with Ziggy the Zebra*.

- **Play Swat the Words.** Find or make an object to use as a swatter, such as a new flyswatter, a plastic ruler, or even just your student's hand. Lay out a selection of Word Cards on the table. Have your student find and swat each card as you read the word aloud. Then switch—you swat while your student reads.

- **Have your student type** a selection of words on the computer. This activity is especially good for kids who struggle with handwriting.

- **Play Word Card Slapjack.** Designate one word as the "jack," and then deal out a stack of cards to two players. Play as you would Slapjack, slapping the "jack" as it comes up. Play several times, changing the "jack" card each time. To make it more challenging, have the student say the word every time he lays down a card.

- **Guess the Word.** Lay down two Word Cards at a time and have your student read one of the cards. You then "guess" which one she read. Be sure to guess wrong now and then! Switch sides and let your student guess which word you read.

- **Use favorite family board games** for Word Card review. Pull out games like Sorry! or Candy Land and have each player read a word before his or her turn.

- **Play Word Card Concentration.** Choose 10-15 review words. Use index cards to make two identical sets of cards, and then play according to the regular rules.

Art and Creative Play

- **Tell a story.** Lay out a selection of review words and have your student make up a silly story using all the words. It's okay if it doesn't make sense; in fact, it probably won't!

- **Illustrate the words.** Select a few words and have your student draw a picture for each one. She may then make a collage of the words and pictures.

- **Color it.** Look for coloring book pages with big spaces and write review words in those spaces. Have the student read each word. If read correctly, she may color that space. Continue until the picture is complete.

- **Use Ziggy activities** from the *All About Reading* Pre-reading program, such as having Ziggy read the words incorrectly so your student can correct him, or having Ziggy read the first sound and the student read the second sound.

- **Glue the Feed the Monster graphic** to an empty cereal box and cut a hole where the mouth is. Have your student read the Word Cards and feed them to the monster. You might also use the monster box as an alternative storage place for the mastered cards.

- **Create a colorful word cloud.** Choose a selection of review words and have your student write each one several times, each time using a different color marker. Create the cloud on a light-colored piece of construction paper. Encourage your student to vary the direction and size of each word.

Snacks and Rewards

- **Snack stacks.** Select 15 review words and place them in five piles of three in front of your student. Place some chocolate chips, marshmallows, M&Ms, popcorn, granola, fruit, or other favorite treat behind each stack of cards. Have your student choose a stack and read the words. If she reads them correctly, she may enjoy the snack from that stack. Continue until all the words have been read correctly, and all the snacks eaten!

- **Play Yucky Snacks.** Select 15 review words and have your student use them to make up "Silly Recipes for Yucky Snacks." For example, the recipe might be to add three cups of *grass*, mix in a tablespoon of *rat*, and garnish with some *bells*. Don't forget to have your student name her creation at the end—and then go make a *real* snack to celebrate.

APPENDIX I
List of Comprehension Activities

Pre- and post-reading comprehension activities are included in every story-related lesson in Level 1. Depending on your student's needs and interests, you may choose to use additional activities.

Pre-Reading Discussions and Activities

- Before your student reads, skim the story and note possible **vocabulary** words your student may not know. Introduce them briefly before your student reads the story.

- Activate prior knowledge by asking one or two questions related to the story. For example, a question for "Fox in a Box" might be: Have you ever played with or made something out of an empty box? Follow the questions with a brief discussion of your student's experiences.

- Show the title page. Based on the title and any illustration that appears there, discuss what the story might be about.

- Make predictions about the story by asking a story-specific question. For example, questions for "The Bat and King Sam" might include: What do you think might happen if a lonely king met a bat in his castle? Do you think they would be friends?

- Discuss the **setting** of the story. If the story is set in a new or unusual place, use a globe or map to introduce the place to your student.

- Relate the story to your student's experience. Questions you might ask include: Have you ever helped a friend solve a problem? Has anyone ever told you that you're too young or too small to do something? Questions may also be story-specific: What are some reasons you might not want an ox in your house? What would you do if it happened?

- Introduce any **literary devices** used in the story, such as onomatopoeia, alliteration, and rhyme. Have your student watch for these devices while reading the story.

Post-Reading Discussions and Activities

- Discuss the **main character** of the story. Who is the main character in this story? Why? What is the character's problem? How does he feel about it? What does he do about it? How does he feel by the end of the story? How has he changed?

- Discuss the main **conflict** of the story. What problem does the main character face? What does the character do to solve the conflict? Does the character's solution work? What would you have done if you were the character?

- Practice meaningful expression. When reading **dialogue**, demonstrate for your student how you can change your tone of voice to reflect how the character is feeling. For example, if the character is scared, you could read "Yuck! I am not fond of cobwebs!" in a scared voice. Then let the student give it a try.

- Skim through the story and ask comprehension questions that require more than a yes or no answer. Types of questions you might ask include: Why do you think the character said that? Does the character look upset or happy? What does your face look like when you're upset? Why do you think the character did that? What happened after the character left home?

- Have your student skim the story for information about a question you ask. For example, a question for "Yuck!" might be: What are the things that Tam is not fond of?

- Relate the story to your student's experience. Questions you might ask include: What would you do if you were this character? How would you solve the problem? What are some things you could do to cheer up a friend (or help someone in danger, or make a nice lunch, and so on)?

- Connect the story to other literature the student has read. Talk about similarities in **theme**, conflict, setting, or character between stories.

- Imagine an alternate ending for the story. For example, questions for "No Mud for Max" might include: What would have happened if Max's friends hadn't come to help him? How would that have changed the outcome of the story?

- Practice story **sequencing**. Choose three action sentences from the story and write them on separate slips of paper. Have your student read the sentences and place them in the correct order as they happened in the story.

- List similarities and differences between characters or settings in the story. For setting, the student could also compare the story setting to his own location.

- Discuss how authors often use the five senses of sight, hearing, touch, smell, and taste in their writing. Encourage your student to go back through the story and point out places that appeal to any of the senses.

- Talk about realism and fantasy. Which parts of the story could have happened? Which parts could not have happened? Why?

Appendix I: List of Comprehension Activities

APPENDIX J
If Your Student Struggles with the Stories

Do any of these situations sound familiar?

- Your student has trouble reading an entire story in one sitting.
- Your student sees how many pages a story is and feels discouraged before he begins.
- Your student has a decoding special need.

If so, it's important to be proactive and tackle the problem head-on so you can maintain your student's motivation to read. Here are some suggestions.

- **Review.** Spend more time reviewing with the flashcards, activities, and Practice Sheets before reading the story. The more familiar the student is with the words, the easier it will be to read the story.

- **Set a timer.** Have your student read until the timer goes off. Choose the length of time according to your student's ability. You may need to start with a short time such as three minutes, and then gradually build up to ten minutes.

- **Divide the story into two or three parts.** Have your student read just one section in a sitting. Bookmark the page. At the next reading session, have your student listen as you reread the part he has already read, and then have him continue reading on his own.

- **Reread.** Rereading stories from previous lessons will help your student gain fluency.

- **Try buddy reading.** Split up the reading duties by reading with your student. Alternate pages by reading a page yourself and then having your student read the next. For even more practice, you might read the story three times by buddy reading twice, switching the pages you each read, and having your student read the story on his own the third time.

  Younger students may enjoy buddy reading with Ziggy the Zebra puppet or another favorite puppet or stuffed animal.

- **Practice blending to eliminate word guessing.** Sometimes students struggle because they guess at words rather than try to decode them. The best solution for word guessing is to use the blending (or decoding) procedure in Appendix C.

- **Check for vision problems.** Be alert to vision problems that may be interfering with your student's ability to read fluently. Some signs to look out for include:
  - frequent eye rubbing, blinking, or squinting
  - short attention span
  - avoiding reading and other close activities
  - frequent headaches
  - covering one eye
  - tilting the head to one side
  - holding reading materials close to the face
  - an eye turning in or out
  - seeing double
  - losing place when reading
  - difficulty remembering what he or she read

Methods for Counting Syllables

Knowing how to recognize and count syllables is an important part of your student's reading progress, and is immensely useful when it comes to decoding words.

If your student needs help with counting syllables, choose one of the engaging methods below.

The Hum Method	Say the word.	Hum each syllable.	*el – e – phant* (hum) (hum) (hum)
The Clap Method	Say the word.	Clap each syllable.	*win – dow* (clap) (clap)
The Robot Method	Say the word in a robotic tone.	Listen to the separation of the word chunks.	*pres – i – dent* (pause) (pause)
The Jump Method	Say the word.	Jump on each syllable.	*mon – key* (jump) (jump)
The Name Method	Say your student's name.	Emphasize each syllable.	*Em – i – ly* *Cae – den* *Mad – i – son* *Bryce*

Magnet Board Setup at the End of Level 1

In Level 1, your student will learn the 26 alphabet phonograms as well as six consonant team phonograms. Add the letter tiles to your magnetic white board as they are taught, and as indicated in the lessons.

At the end of Level 1, your white board will look like the illustration below. This is also how your white board will be set up when you begin Level 2.

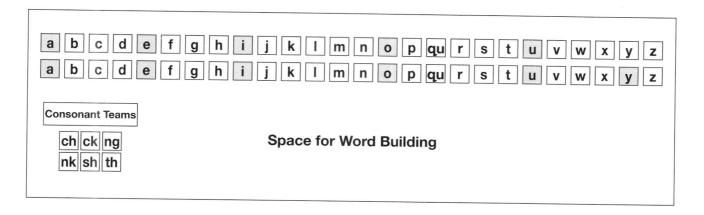

In future levels, more letter tiles will be added to the board, organized under the following labels:

| Vowel Teams | The Sound of /er/ | The Sound of /sh/ | Other Tiles |

APPENDIX M
Leap Words Taught in Level 1

Leap Words are high-frequency words that either don't follow the normal rules or contain phonograms that your student hasn't practiced yet. Your student will be "leaping ahead" to learn these words as sight words. They are indicated on the Word Cards by the leaping frog.

Leap Words comprise a small percentage of the words taught in Level 1. Out of 193 words taught, only 11 are Leap Words.

Leap Word	Lesson	Why Taught as a Leap Word
the	2	The most common pronunciation, /thŭ/, is not phonetic.
a	6	The most common pronunciation, /ŭ/, is not phonetic.
of	10	The o says its fourth sound, which hasn't been taught yet. The f says /v/ instead of /f/ like we would expect.
was	24	The a says /ŭ/, which isn't one of its typical sounds.
to	26	The o says its third sound, which hasn't been taught yet.
said	29	The ai says /ĕ/, which isn't one of its typical sounds.
I	29	The long i sound hasn't been taught yet.
or	31	Phonogram or hasn't been taught yet.
for	31	Phonogram or hasn't been taught yet.
no	31	The o says its second sound, which hasn't been taught yet.
do	40	The o says its third sound, which hasn't been taught yet.

Words Taught in Level 1

The number listed corresponds with the lesson in which the word is first introduced.

A

a. 6
act 24
ad. 4
add. 29
Alps 42
am 1
an. 2
and. 24
Ann 29
ant 24
anthill 40
anthills 42
as 12
Ash 20
ash 20
ask 24
at 2
ax 16

B

back. 34
backdrop 40
backlog 40
backpack 40
bad. 4
bag. 4
bam 2
ban. 2
band. 24
bang. 36
bank. 38
banks 42
bash 20
bask 24
bat 2
bath 18
bathtub 40
bathtubs. 42
be. 52
bed. 14
bedbug. 40
bedbugs 42
beg. 14
bell. 29
bells 42
belt. 24
belts 42
Ben 14
bench. 24
benches 42
bend. 24
bent 24
Bess 29
best 24
bet 14
Beth. 18

Bev. 14
bid 8
big 8
Bill. 29
bill 29
bin 8
bit 8
black 34
blacktop. 40
blank 38
blink 38
bliss 29
blob 26
block 34
blot 26
bluff. 29
blush 26
blushes. 42
Bob 10
bobcat 40
bobcats. 42
bog. 10
bond 24
bop. 10
boss 29
box. 16
boxes 42
Brad. 26
brag 26
bran 26
brass. 29
Bret 26
brick. 34
bricks 42
brim 26
bring 36
broth 26
brush 26
brushes. 42
buck. 34
buckskin 34
bud. 12
Bud 12
bug. 12
bulk 24
bump 24
bun 12
bunch. 24
bunk. 38
bunkbed. 40
bus 12
but 12
buzz. 29
buzzes 42

C

cab 4

Cal. 10
camp 24
can 4
cannot 40
Cap 4
cap 4
cash 20
cashbox 40
cast. 24
castoff 40
cat 4
cats. 42
catfish 40
catnip. 40
cats. 42
Chad 22
chaff 29
champ 24
chap 22
chat 22
check 34
checklist. 40
checks 42
chess 29
Chet. 22
chick 34
chill 29
chills 42
chimp. 24
chin 22
Chip 22
chip 22
chomp 24
chomps 42
chop. 22
chopstick 40
chopsticks 42
chuck. 34
chug. 22
chum 22
chunk. 38
clad 26
clam 26
clamshell 40
clang 36
clank 38
clap 26
clash. 26
clashes 42
class 29
classes 42
Clem 26
click. 34
cliff 29
cling. 36
clink. 38
clip. 26

clock 34
clocks. 42
cloth. 26
club 26
cluck 34
clung 36
clunk 38
cobweb. 40
cobwebs 42
cod. 10
codfish 40
cop. 10
cost 24
cot 10
crab 26
crack 34
cram. 26
crank 38
crash 26
crashes 42
cress 29
crib. 26
crop 26
cross. 29
crosswind. 40
crush 26
cub. 12
cud. 12
cuff 29
cup. 12
cut 12

D

dab. 4
dad. 4
damp 24
Dan 4
dash 20
dashes 42
Deb 14
deck. 34
Del. 14
den. 14
dent 24
desk. 24
desks 42
desktop 40
Dex 16
did 8
dig 8
dim 8
ding 36
dip 8
dish 20
dishes. 42
dishcloth 40
dishpan 40

dishpans 42	fishes 42	go 52	hotspot 40
disk 24	fist 24	gob 10	huff 29
do 40	fit 8	gong 36	hug 12
Doc 10	fix 16	got 10	hugs 42
dock 34	fixes 42	grab 26	hum 12
dog 10	fizz 29	gram 26	hump 24
doll 29	fizzes 42	grass 29	humpback 40
Don 10	flag 26	Greg 26	hung 36
dot 10	flags 42	grid 26	hunk 38
Dot 10	flank 38	grim 26	hunt 24
drab 26	flap 26	grin 26	hush 20
drag 26	flapjack 40	grip 26	husk 24
drank 38	flapjacks 42	grit 26	hut 12
dress 29	flash 26	grub 26	
dresses 42	flashes 42	gruff 29	**I**
drill 29	flat 26	gull 29	I 29
drink 38	fleck 34	gulp 24	ick 34
drip 26	fled 26	gum 12	if 8
drop 26	flick 34	gumdrop 40	ill 29
drug 26	fling 36	Gump 24	in 8
drum 26	flip 26	gun 12	inch 24
drumstick 40	flit 26	gunshot 40	ink 38
duck 34	flock 34	Gus 12	inkblot 40
duct 24	flop 26	gush 20	inkblots 42
dug 12	floss 29	gust 24	inkjet 40
dump 24	fluff 29		inkwell 40
dunk 38	flung 36	**H**	inn 29
dusk 24	flunk 38	had 6	into 40
dust 24	flush 26	ham 6	is 12
dustbin 40	flushes 42	hand 24	it 8
dustpan 40	fog 10	handbag 40	itself 40
	fond 24	handcuff 40	
E	for 31	handgun 40	**J**
Ed 14	fox 14	handheld 40	jab 2
egg 29	foxes 42	hang 36	Jack 34
eggnog 40	Fran 26	Hank 38	jam 2
eggshell 40	Frank 38	has 12	Jan 2
elf 24	Fred 26	hash 20	Jax 16
elk 24	fresh 26	hat 6	jazz 29
elm 24	frog 26	he 52	Jeb 14
end 24	fun 12	held 24	Jed 14
	fund 24	help 24	Jeff 29
F	fuss 29	hem 14	Jen 14
fact 24	fusses 42	hen 14	Jess 29
fad 8	fuzz 29	hens 42	jest 24
fan 8		hi 52	jet 14
fang 36	**G**	hid 8	jig 8
fast 24	gal 10	hill 29	Jill 29
fat 8	gang 36	hilltop 40	Jim 8
fax 16	gap 4	hilltops 42	job 10
fed 14	gas 4	him 8	jog 10
fell 29	gash 20	himself 40	Jon 10
felt 24	gasp 24	hint 24	Josh 20
fend 24	get 14	hip 8	jug 12
fest 24	gift 24	his 12	jump 24
fig 8	Gil 8	hiss 29	junk 38
fill 29	glad 26	hisses 42	just 24
film 24	glass 29	hit 8	jut 12
filth 24	glasses 42	hog 10	
fin 8	Glen 26	honk 38	**K**
finch 24	glob 26	honks 42	Ken 14
Finn 29	glop 26	hop 10	Kent 24
fish 20	glum 26	hot 10	kept 24

Appendix N: Words Taught in Level 1

kick 34
kid 8
kill 29
Kim 8
king 36
kings. 42
Kip. 8
kiss. 29
kisses. 42

L
lack. 34
lad 10
lamp. 24
lamps 42
land 24
lap 10
laptop. 40
lash 20
last 24
lax 16
led 14
left 24
leg 14
lend 24
lent. 24
less 29
let. 14
lick. 34
lid 10
lift 24
Lill. 29
limp 24
Ling. 36
lint 24
lip 10
lipstick 40
lisp 24
list 24
lit 10
Liv 10
Liz 10
lock 34
locks. 42
locksmith 40
loft 24
log 10
long 36
loss. 29
lost 24
lot 10
luck 34
lug 12
lump 24
lunch 24
lung 36

M
Mac 4
mad 4
man 2
map 1
mash 20

mask 24
mast 24
mat 2
math 18
Matt 29
Max 16
me 52
Meg 14
Mel 14
meld. 24
melt 24
men 14
mend 24
mess. 29
messes 42
met 14
milk 24
milkman 40
mill 29
Ming 36
mint 24
miss 29
Miss. 29
misses 42
mist 24
mix. 16
mixes 42
mob 10
mock 34
mom 10
mop 10
moss. 29
moth 18
much 22
muck 34
mud 12
muff. 29
mug 12
mulch. 24
mum 12
munch 24
munches 42
mush 20
musk 24
muskrat 40
must. 24

N
nab. 2
Nan 2
nap. 2
Nat 2
neck. 34
Ned 14
Nell 29
nest 24
net 14
next 24
Nick. 34
nip 8
no 31
nod. 10
not. 10

nut. 12
nutshell. 40
nutshells. 42

O
odd 29
of. 10
off 29
offset 40
on 10
onto 40
or 31
ox. 16

P
pack. 34
pad 4
padlock 40
pal 10
Pam 1
pan 2
panfish. 40
pang. 36
pant 24
pass 29
passes. 42
past 24
pat 2
Pat 2
path 18
peck 34
Peg. 14
pen. 14
pest 24
pet 14
pets 42
pick 34
pig 8
pigpen 40
pill 29
pin 8
pinch 24
ping 36
pink 38
Pip. 8
pit 8
plan 26
plank 38
plod 26
plop 26
plot 26
plots. 42
pluck 34
plug 26
plum 26
plunk 38
plus 26
pod. 10
pond 24
pop. 10
popgun. 40
pot 10
prank 38

press. 29
presses 42
prick. 34
prim. 26
prop. 26
puff 29
pug. 12
pump 24
pun 12
punch. 24
punt 24
pup. 12

Q
quack 34
quacks 42
quest 24
quick 34
quicksand. 40
quill 29
quills 42
quilt 24
Quinn 29
quit 14
quiz 16

R
rack 34
raft. 24
rag 6
ram 6
ramp 24
ran 6
ranch 24
rang 36
rank 38
rant 24
rap 6
rash 20
rashes 42
rasp. 24
rat 6
red 14
rent 24
rest. 24
rib 8
rich 22
riches 42
Rick. 34
rid 8
rig 8
rim 8
ring 36
rink. 38
rip 8
risk. 24
rob 10
Rob 10
rock 34
rod 10
romp 24
Ron 10
Ross. 29

– NOTES –